Byron and Scotland
Radical or Dandy?

Frontispiece: George Sanders' portrait of Byron landing from a boat, reproduced by gracious permission of H.M. the Queen

Byron and Scotland

Radical or Dandy?

edited by
ANGUS CALDER

EDINBURGH UNIVERSITY PRESS

© Edinburgh University Press 1989
22 George Square, Edinburgh

Set in Linotron Palatino
by Hewer Text Composition Services, Edinburgh
and printed in Great Britain by
Redwood Burn Limited
Trowbridge, Wilts

British Library Cataloguing
    in Publication Data
Byron & Scotland: radical or dandy?
1. Poetry in English. Byron, George Gordon Byron.
Baron 1788–1824
I. Calder, Angus
821'.7
ISBN 0 85224 618 8
ISBN 0 85224 651 X pbk

Contents

Contributors

SHEENA BLACKHALL is a North East Scot, who has written four collections of poetry, and a volume of Scots short stories. A further collection of poems, and another short story volume, are due to be published later this year. A single parent, she is a ballad-singer, poet, writer, and illustrator.

DRUMMOND BONE is Lecturer in English Literature at the University of Glasgow. From 1979 until 1988 he was the academic editor of *The Byron Journal*, and he wrote the Romantic Poetry section of *The Years Work in English Studies* from 1985–87. He has lectured on Byron in most European countries, in the middle East and in India. Alongside his articles on Romanticism he also writes his own fiction.

NORMAN BUCHAN, a Labour MP since 1964, now represents Paisley South. He was a Minister in two Labour Governments and has held several 'shadow' positions including Arts and Media. He is a frequent contributor to political and cultural journals. He is the editor of 'The Scottish Folksinger' and '101 Scottish Songs.' He is Chairman of the Tribune Board.

DAVID CRAIG, born in Aberdeen, is Senior Lecturer in Creative Writing, School of Creative Arts, University of Lancaster. His latest published book *Native Stones* is being followed by one on oral memories of the Highland Clearances.

ANGUS CALDER is Reader in Literature and Cultural Studies and Staff Tutor in Arts, Open University in Scotland. He has written works of history (*The People's War: Britain 1939–45* and *Revolutionary Empire: The Rise of the English-Speaking Empires from the Fifteenth Century to the 1780s*) literary criticism (of African, Caribbean and Scottish Literature) and a short introduction to *Byron*. He co-edited *Journal of Commonwealth Literature* from 1981 to 1987 and frequently contributes to *London Review of Books, New Statesman, Cencrastus* and *Inter-Arts*.

JON CURT, born in Dundee, is doing a PhD on Byron for the University of Edinburgh and is currently a Lecturer in English at the University of Monastir, Tunisia.

WILLIAM J. DONNELLY obtained his doctorate from the School of Scottish Studies of Edinburgh University. He is a tutor in literature – including Romantic Poetry – with the Open University, author and co-author respectively of two study guides, *Scottish Society and Culture* and *Scottish Literature*, and co-editor, with Angus Calder, of a forthcoming Penguin *Selected Burns*.

DOUGLAS DUNN is a writer and poet. He contributes to *The Glasgow Herald, The New Yorker* and *TLS*. His most recent book of verse is *Northlight* (1988). He is an honorary professor in the University of Dundee.

MARGERY MCCULLOCH is a London graduate and was awarded her doctorate in Scottish Literature by the University of Glasgow. She has written extensively on twentieth-century Scottish Literature and is the author of a critical study of the novels of Neil M. Gunn. Her study of Edwin Muir is due to be published shortly. She is a literature tutor with the Open University and a visiting lecturer in Scottish Literature at the University of Glasgow.

ANDREW NOBLE is Head of the Literature Section in the Department of English Studies at Strathclyde University. He has written extensively on Scottish literature and is presently completing *Robert Burns and the Romantic Revolution* which expands some of the issues present in his Byron essay.

MICHAEL REES has been joint international secretary of The Byron Society since 1982, and was joint chairman 1975–78. Educated at Harrow and Cambridge, he studied in France and Italy and worked for the Wellcome Foundation 1968–88. He is currently translating Countess Teresa Guiccioli's *La Vie de Lord Byron en Italie*.

P. H. SCOTT is Rector of Dundee University. Born and educated in Edinburgh, and after many years abroad as a diplomat, he has been active in Scottish causes and has written extensively on historical, literary and political subjects. Publications include: *1707: The Union of Scotland and England, Walter Scott and Scotland, John Galt, In Bed with an Elephant*.

Preface

NORMAN BUCHAN MP

I was delighted to learn that the Open University and Glasgow University were organizing a symposium on the theme of Byron and Scotland. I was even more pleased to know that this book would emerge from the symposium, taking a closer look at the influences of Scotland and Byron, each upon the other. I declare an interest. I tend to agree with MacDiarmid that Byron was a great Scottish genius, and should be seen as such, despite his various anti-Caledonian strictures. (Perhaps indeed because of them. I have little doubt that he would have merrily helped to strangle the last Free Kirk Minister with the last copy of the *Sunday Post*!) In any case we cannot have better authority than Byron himself: he was, he said, half-Scot by birth and bred a whole one.

Nor is this is merely because of his origins, about which from time to time – notably at the Byron Bicentenary Dinner – we have had to give a mild corrective reminder. No, it is because there is a curiously Scottish hardheadedness, a permanent objective self-mockery that marks him out from almost all of his English literary contemporaries. His Romanticism for example is not that of Wordsworth. Imagine Wordsworth part of an Edinburgh scene – drinking in a contemporary howff in the High Street or in a pub in Rose Street in more recent times. For all his apparent English milordism, Byron, I suspect, would have been at home. And of course he was affected by his childhood. If the Jesuits can claim a seven-year sovereignty for a child, it is a nonsense to dismiss Byron's ten. And what an area to grow up in – singing Aberdeenshire no less.

I have always been struck by one enormous and significant difference between the Scottish (and Irish) poets of the Romantic Revolution and their English contemporaries. In Scotland, all of them, to a greater or lesser extent, were not

only poets but song-writers – Burns, Scott, Hogg, Tannahill . . .
and with a recent continuing ancestry, right back to Alan
Ramsay and the eighteenth century women writers ('Song-
stresses' the book calls them), Baillie and Nairn et al. But in
England, even when they essayed the odd lyric, not one of
them was a song craftsman, a song makar; not Coleridge,
Wordsworth, Southey . . . And to emphasise the point the only
other poet who came near it was, of course, the Irish Thomas
Moore. It is for this reason that I can never dismiss the
Aberdeenshire influence on Byron. Firstly, it clearly exists.
Not just his occasional echoes – 'Lachin Y Gair', for example –
but the more clearly derivative, like his 'So we'll go no more
a-roving.' Hamish Henderson pointed out, in a typically
generous and helpful letter to me, that the opening of that
song, in its ballad form as the chorus of *The Jolly Beggar*, had
already been printed several times before Byron included it
in a letter to Moore from Venice in 1817. It is not therefore
an oral, folk version of the Byron poem. (A phenomenon that
can and does happen.) On the contrary, it is the folk version,
pretty constant in its various forms, that is the origin of the
Byron:

> An' we'll gang nae mair a-rovin'
> Sae late intae the nicht
> We'll gang nae mair a'rovin'
> Though the moon shines ne'er sae bricht.

Hamish Henderson lists at least three examples printed before
1817: in Herd's *Ancient and Modern Scottish Songs* (1776),
Ritson's *Scottish Song* (1794) and, of course, *The Scots Musical
Museum*.

The primacy of the ballad is clear therefore. And it is equally
clear to anyone who knows how these things work, that the
echo is orally derived and not from the printed book. (Though,
as Henderson points out, Byron does make reference to his
awareness of printed balladry in the Introduction to *Childe
Harold*. 'The "Good Night" in the beginning of the first canto',
writes Byron, 'was suggested by "Lord Maxwell's Good
Night" in the Border Minstrelsy, edited by Mr. Scott.') He
liked the song form, as the ease of his lyrics show: 'She Walks

in Beauty', for example. His longer works are frequently punctuated by a lyric, *Childe Harold* and *Don Juan* itself. And in this characteristic the sense of Scottishness goes much deeper than a single remembered throwback to Aberdeenshire.

In the first place, the point about song – as compared to the printed poem – is its immediacy of contact and effect, its social rather than individual audience and therefore its deeply popular, indeed democratic, nature as an art form. And all of that is intensely Scottish – though, thank goodness, not exclusively so – in recent British cultural history. As in the form so, frequently, with the content. Despite its reference point presence in Scottish literary history, Ramsay's gentrified 'Gentle Shepherd' was alien to the surrounding song from which it was derived, which was inevitably popular, and therefore frequently radical.

That last quality is worth stressing. The picture of the gloom and doom Romantic is, of course, long exploded. Byron's hero was Pope. His style was eventually Augustan. He combined the radicalism of song with the brisk thinking-on-your-feet style of oral argument. He continually 'said' something. *Don Juan* is simply the best piece of hard-headed verse journalism we have in English, and at the same time a great and rollicking epic. He was one of the few who have combined coolness with passion. An agnostic who seemed to have respected the Calvinist zeal for argument. He said that as a boy he had read most of the Bible 'through and through – that is to say, the Old Testament, for the New struck me as a task, but the Old as a pleasure. I speak as a boy from the recollected impression of that period at Aberdeen in 1796.' He clearly revelled in the thundering of the language of the old Testament and the debate of the theologians – though he remained a sceptic, a common enough Scottish experience. Here he is in a letter to Edward Noel Long, quoted by Michael Foot in his *Politics of Paradise*: 'This much I will venture to affirm, that all the virtues and pious *Deeds* performed on Earth can never entitle a man to Everlasting happiness in a future State; nor on the other hand can such a Seat of eternal punishment exist . . .' And later, and with the customary wry sting in the tail, he comments: 'In Morality I prefer Confucius to the ten Commandments and

Socrates to St. Paul (even though the two latter agree in their
opinion about marriage)' . . . But he liked the argument and the
passion, and no man could use them better, and since he had
no hope of a spiritual heaven in the hereafter he at least set
about using these twin tools to get rid of a human hell in the
present. In short, he became to his everlasting glory the poet of
Revolution. He sang about it, he joked about it, he argued for it
and ultimately he died for it.

In *Cain*, in *Manfred*, in *Marino Faliero*, he set out his stall.
Man's noblest task was to revolt against tyranny whether of
secular ruler, God or Devil. He seems to have equated the last
two. And, rather like Milton, he gives the devil all the best
lines. To Lucifer in *Cain* for instance:

> Souls who dare use their immortality,
> Souls who dare look the Omnipotent tyrant in
> His everlasting face and tell him that
> His evil is not good!

And here, as in *Manfred*, he hints at the argument that being
given knowledge is not enough – man needs power too. An
interesting and never properly examined shift from the Faust
of Marlowe and perhaps also of Goethe. A comment on the
insufficiency of the Liberal (bourgeois) revolution? I offer that
idea freely to someone for a doctoral thesis! (preferably, I can
hear Byron say, in Theology.) In *Marino Faliero*, above all, the
theme of revolution is made clear. Indeed at times he theorises
on the very nature of revolt. His analysis of the ambivalent
position of the aristocrat Faliero himself, as he throws in his lot
with the revolutionaries to destroy the Senate, must come
close to Byron's own position. And it is the weakness of Faliero
as opposed to the hardened revolutionaries, Bertuccio and
Calendaro, which exposes their plot, leads to their common
defeat and the ultimate execution of Faliero.

The last scene takes place in the centre of the courtyard of
the Doge's Palace, with Faliero on the scaffold. The people,
vaguely heard in the distance, are locked outside the gates
watching the execution. He asks to speak and is told the
people are too far away. They cannot hear him. The whole
scene curiously echoes an earlier scene when one of the

conspirators asks: 'But if we fail . . .?' And Bertuccio replies: 'They never fail who die/In a great cause: the block may soak their gore;/. . . But still their spirit walks abroad. Though years/Elapse and others share as dark a doom,/They but augment the deep and sweeping thoughts/Which overpower all others, and conduct/The world at last to freedom.' In the same way, Faliero speaks unheard and says: 'I speak to time and to eternity . . .' Then, in an extraordinarily modernist way, the entire action of the execution scene is repeated once more, with a different perspective both of location and mood. This time the scene is enacted from outside the locked gates and from among the crowd. As they watch the execution, the people murmur of continuing revolt. (In modern Venetian terms,' la lotta continua!') 'Then they have murdered him who have freed us . . . we would have brought/Weapons, and forced them! 'and as the gates open and the crowd rush in, the curtain falls. I know of no comparable technical experiment like this until our own century, in the Japanese film *Rashomon*, for example. Regrettably, Byron, who described the play, in self-comparison with Napoleon, as his 'Leipzig', forbade its production in his own time. (Though it was, I believe, performed once in the Green Room at Drury Lane, against his wishes.)

We need not wonder at Byron's identification with revolution. His Scottish mother (one of the 'mad Gordons of Gight') was herself a fairly outspoken radical. Writing in 1792, in the middle of the wildest anti-French Revolution hysteria, she remarked calmly: '. . . I do not think the King. [i.e. King Louis XVI] after his treachery and perjury, deserves to be restored. To be sure there has been horrid things done by the People, but if the other party had been successful, there would have been as great cruelty committed by them . . .' And she goes on to refer with some interest to the formation of the Friends of the People in the principal towns of Scotland.

And not for nothing was Byron often identified in the public mind with King Ludd himself. Writing at a time when we have witnessed the nobility of the realm summoned in their hundreds to pass a Poll Tax that benefitted all of them at the expense of the mass of the people, we can guess at how Byron might have flayed them. Indeed we have evidence. He spoke three times in the House of Lords, each time with courage and each time for freedom. The nobleman speaking for the poor mechanic. The agnostic speaking for Catholic freedom. Even allowing for the rhetoric of the time his speech attacking the Bill to bring in the death penalty against the machine-breakers rings tough and hard. And it remains worth the quoting. He had not long returned to England from his travels in the Balkans, which he compared with what he was now witnessing in England:

I have been in some of the most oppressed provinces of Turkey. But never under the most despotic of infidel governments did I behold such squalid wretchedness as I have seen since my return in the very heart of a Christian country. And what are your remedies? After months of inaction, and months of action worse than inactivity, at length comes forth the grand specific, the never failing nostrum of all state physicians . . . the warm water of your mawkish police and the lancets of your military. . . . How will you carry your Bill into effect? Can you commit a whole county to their own prisons? Will you erect a gibbet in every field and hang up men like scarecrows? . . . Are these the remedies for a starving and desperate people? When a proposal is made to emancipate or relieve, you hesitate, you deliberate for years; but a Death Bill must be passed off-hand without a thought for the consequences.

And even if it were passed, he said, even with all the battery of powers in the Bill, 'It would still need two things more – Twelve butchers for a jury, and a Jeffreys for a judge!'

Then all of this – the direct commitment to political involvement, the humour and the passion, the directness of song, his glorying in rhyme and rhythm – came together. He was working on a new poem, he told Moore. It was a bit facetious, but even so it might be 'too free for these very modest times'. Gone the occasional posturing, the mock romantic, the overstrained language of his dramas. In its place the marvellous stanza form of *Don Juan*, carrying what Michael Foot calls the 'Politics of Paradise' in a seemingly unending flow of invention, witty, sharp, confident, his passion for liberty, sharpened by his love for Italy (and Teresa Guiccioli), his hatred of tyrants, now clearer as he moved away from his ambivalence about Napoleon. And through it all a happier and easier narrative line than exists anywhere else in English-language poetry – not Pope, not Dryden, not Scott. It has a kind of artlessness at variance with the enormous skill even of the rhyming techniques. Only in the very different verse form of the ballad do we find this same colloquial ease. (Perhaps also in the Burns of 'Tam o' Shanter' and he, of course, was steeped in ballad and song.) Perhaps 'singing Aberdeenshire' influenced him more than he knew – or we can know. (He remembered enough to call the Grammar School the 'squeel'.)

Don Juan was an enormous achievement. It remains a masterpiece. All the old targets all there, but his stance is cool and his aim sharpened. God or evil man together:

> 'Let there be light!' said God and there was light,
> 'Let there be blood!' said man, and there's a sea!

Through all the fun and the sex and the vitriol of *Don Juan*, there remains a conscious combining purpose. He is comment-ing on the world, as a kind of merry didactic journalist – and *that's* certainly a Scottish trait. But so is the radical heart of the message:

> For I will teach, if possible, the stones
> To rise against Earth's tyrants. Never let it
> Be said that we still truckle unto thrones –
> But ye, our children's children! think how we
> Showed what things were before the world was free!

I wish this book well. It is timely, following Byron's bicenten-ary year. And even more timely, perhaps, because of the moral and intellectual climate we presently endure. When even the work of Lord Elgin has still to be dealt with, and restitution made to Greece.

For the spoken and the written word is under attack again as it was with Byron. We are facing an indirect but comprehensive and increasing censorship. His publisher, Murray, seemed timid enough to Byron. His correspondence is full of complaints about it. But would similar work, taking on latter-day Castlereaghs or Prince Regents, find any readier a publisher today? In Byron's time and after, seven hundred men, women and children went to gaol for distributing the unstamped press – The Poor Men's Guardians. Today the popular press is in the hands of only three men: Maxwell, Murdoch and Stevens. The government pursues across five continents, and with all the dented majesty of the law, an old man's book on his disreputable trade of spying. We have restored a *de facto* Lord Chamberlain in the shape of Rees-Mogg. The freedom of the broadcaster is under attack and badly dented after 'Real Lives', 'Zircon' and the invasion of Scottish BBC by the Special Branch. Self-censorship has lowered the threshold at which censorship begins. Clause 28 would endanger a contemporary Byron. A new Obscenity Act is threatened and with it all the joyous life of a modern rhyming *Don Juan* would be in jeopardy.

What red meat all this would be to Byron! How he would have scarified the visit of a premier to the General Assembly! The evocation of St Paul, of Christ, of God! All that and *The Sunday Times*, too – how could he have resisted it? The memory of his *English Bards and Scotch Reviewers* . . . perhaps an English Bird and Scottish Prelates? The combination would have been irresistible!

No. He would certainly have written it. But in today's developing climate, would he, could he, have found a publisher brave enough to publish him?

Introduction

ANGUS CALDER

Of the dozen contributors to this volume, all but one are Scots. The occasion which brought us together was a Conference on 'Byron and Scotland' organised in January 1988 to celebrate the bicentenary of Byron's birth, by myself and Peter Gilmour on behalf of the Open University and Ann Karkalas for the Department of Adult and Continuing Education of Glasgow University, which provided the venue.

As organisers, we aimed to put on something which would involve well-equipped specialists in Byron and in Scottish literature but would be 'open' to any of the enquiring adults who provide a clientèle for our month-in month-out activities. The atmosphere was deliberately informal. A session addressed by David Craig and Andrew Noble generated particularly vigorous debate, in which Norman Buchan MP intervened on lines suggested by the Preface which he has kindly contributed to this volume. Proceedings concluded with a reading by Douglas Dunn, an award-winning Scottish poet who has edited Byron, and Sheena Blackhall, who not only writes verse in the Aberdeenshire Doric which Byron heard around him in his childhood, but sings unaccompanied in the North-Eastern tinker tradition.

So, the vitality of the occasion was drawn not only from its topic, but from the current resurgence of Scottish culture, involved as it has been with passionate politics. When Saintsbury and Grierson, to whom Jon Curt refers in his contribution, were professors at Edinburgh University, Scottish literature was regarded as an annexe to English. Very few well-read people in Scotland see it that way now. The independent Scottish tradition, which T. S. Eliot, writing on Byron in the 1930s, perceived, albeit rather dimly, is now recognised as something which from Barbour to the present

1

day has created its own characteristic modes of address to the reader, its own complex of intertextualities. No one in their senses would claim that this tradition wholly determined Byron's writing, but only a very obtuse person could miss the signs that his Scottish childhood left a strange mark on him, or fail to see some significance in his eager appreciation of Burns and Scott, poets who demonstrably influenced him.

His work, of course, has to be seen in relationship to other traditions. Jerome McGann's wonderful notes to his new definitive edition of the *Poetical Works* demonstrate Byron's saturation in the heritage of classical literature which he shared with every well-educated Scottish, English or European contemporary. Italy gave him the stanza form which he used in his finest work. His veneration of Pope and his commitment to Popeian satire help to explain certain scathing passages about Scotland and Scots to which Douglas Dunn draws attention in this volume. Pope's most notable successor had been Charles Churchill. In the phase of intense anti-Scottishness directed at the person of Lord Bute, George III's Prime Minister, Churchill's *Prophecy of Famine* (1763) had been lavish with invective. The Scottish landscape, for instance, had been described thus:

> Far as the eye could reach, no tree was seen,
> Earth, clad in russet, scorn'd the lively green:
> The plague of locusts they secure defy,
> For in three hours a grasshopper must die . . .

Innovative though he was elsewhere in form and feeling, Byron wrote couplet-satire as a follower of Pope and Churchill, and I think *English Bards and Scotch Reviewers* and *The Curse of Minerva* reveal no serious anti-Scottish animus, rather a young poet's emulation of his predecessor: he drew from a bank of anti-Caledonian jibes.

Likewise, it can be argued that his famous House of Lords speeches exhibit a young Whig striving to imitate the admired effects of Fox, Sheridan, Erskine. I see no reason to dispute Malcolm Kelsall's assertion in his recent *Byron's Politics* (1987, p.2) that Byron inherited the tradition of 'the patrician Whigs' and that, like his friends Hobhouse and Kinnaird, he was self-consciously a would-be successor to the late, great Charles James Fox. He was not a democrat. He had a Whiggish horror of mob rule, though he shared the Whig belief that men had a right to use arms to preserve themselves and their liberty. Hence his admiration for Washington, the Republican slave-holder, was not self-contradictory, and hence Pushkin and his aristocratic Decembrist friends were right to sense a fellow-spirit in him. But does his aristocratical Whiggery account fully for the power of his best political verse? Was he, in spite of his cooler judgement, a revolutionary writer of democratical tendency? Our volume opens with Norman Buchan's impassioned claims for Byron's radicalism, and the intriguing link which he makes between this and the Scottish song tradition. David Craig, on the other hand, views him in the context of English radicalism, and attributes the 'shallowness' of all but his best verse to his remoteness from the popular movement. Andrew Noble goes further to accuse Byron of 'collusion' with his purported audience, of creating fluent trash, and of exemplifying, with his 'displaced nationalism', the capitulation of Scottish culture to Unionism and Imperialism, – and yet acknowledges the 'archetypal Scottish Calvinist' who wrote a masterpiece in *Don Juan*.

The interesting – indeed, all-important – question of Byron's religious perspectives proved harder to expose at our conference than problems to do with politics, class and nationality. For far too long the Scottish literary intelligentsia have tended to assume that our nation's Christian inheritance is a Bad Thing, typified by bigotry, joylessness, betrayal (the supposed role of the Church in the Clearances) and, latterly, the prudery of Roman priests. Dr Donnelly's contribution on 'Byron and Catholicism' is especially welcome in that it takes seriously the weight of Calvinism's perfectly logical presentation of the unsaved individual, and humanity in general, as 'uncatered for, unreconciled, irredeemable', and the pressure which it put on Byron, so helping to explain what is otherwise a puzzle, this pre-eminently 'Freethinking' poet's attraction to Catholic ritual and the Catholic concept of Purgatory.

The traditions of the Gordons of Gight were Catholic. From

Jenny Wormald's admirable *Court, Kirk and Community: Scotland 1470–1625* (1981, pp133–4) we learn that in 1610 the Protestant Bishop of Moray 'wrote a moving letter to King James pleading that the Catholic Laird of Gight should be left in peace because he was ill . . . "the papists, I perceive, are not universally of ane corrupt disposition".' The surprising tolerance which characterised Scottish society in the first few decades after the Reformation has been overlaid by images of the Covenanting period which followed – yet it helps to explain the persistence of a folk culture in which James' great Catholic court-poet, Montgomerie, was read and revered while gentry and peasantry alike preserved and extended the national heritage of song. The supposed meanness of the Scot, denounced by Churchill and others and still part of our image abroad, is belied by the generosity of feeling in that heritage.

Byron could be intensely snobbish: the posture went with his romanticisation of his ancient lineage, his elevation of Pope and contempt for Wordsworth, and his dislike (not merely paranoid, in view of the extreme penalties which his homosexuality might have incurred) of the Evangelical morality of the English middle and, in some part, lower classes. But the claim that he was a democrat in spite of himself could (perhaps) be based on the generosity, the human fellow feeling, which he extends in *Don Juan* to people of all nations and classes. A similar quality was present in the writings of Walter Scott. Paul Scott's very thorough investigation here of his great namesake's relations with Byron shows both men in an excellent light.

Margery McCulloch's study of the dealings of another major Scottish novelist, John Galt, with 'the Noble Lord', illuminates both writers. It also brings out the point – obvious enough, when one thinks of it – that in that heyday of British expansion, in which Scots joined so avidly, one did not have to visit Scotland in order to meet plenty Scots. Douglas Kinnaird, Byron's intimate friend, banker and financial adviser was like himself of noble Scottish antecedents. Douglas Dunn's review of Byron's concern over the 'Marbles' riven from the Parthenon by another wandering Scot, Lord Elgin, illuminates European vistas in which Scots intruded themselves everywhere and raises again the question of 'displaced nationalism', a matter which I address, though not directly, in my own contribution on *The Island*.

The popular verse narratives of the Romantic heyday cry out to be decoded in terms of political ideology. Scottish practitioners of the genre were paramount – and Walter Scott, Thomas Campbell and Byron were all intensely 'political' people. It is my own conviction that the specific characteristics of *Scottish* romanticism could bear a lot more investigation, and that Byron's now unfashionable verse tales might be found to share in them. Meanwhile, Drummond Bone takes further than most have done the interesting but painful process of probing minutely into the presences and absences in Romantic literature which accompanied the evolution of a nostalgic, tartan-patterned image of Scotland for home and foreign consumption.

Mercifully, Scottish culture has had enough vitality to defeat the stereotypers and nostalgia-mongers. Sheena Blackhall writes from a North-Eastern milieu of literature and song which, more than any regional culture in Britain, has retained continuity and self-sufficiency. The fact that a poem by local-boy Byron is sung in Aberdeen as if it had no author but the people points to an enduring characteristic of Scottish literature: the closeness of our greatest writers to the everyday life around them. MacDiarmid's posture as a self-confessed élitist is *not* an exception that proves the rule, since his élitism was expressed, paradoxically, in demotic terms. I don't myself care very much whether Englishpersons or other foreigners choose to regard Byron as a Scottish writer: I do heartily hope that many more Scots will come to feel, as I do, that the author of *Don Juan* is as close to us as 'Davie' Lyndsay and 'Rabbie' Burns. As Scotland seeks to express its identity within the structure of the European Community, to be strengthened in 1992, the Aberdeen boy who loved Italy and died in Greece might seem an especially apt culture-hero.

Byron the Radical

DAVID CRAIG

In Aberdeen forty or fifty years ago Byron was very much 'our poet'. My grandfather had had a bronze statue of him placed on a granite tower in front of the Grammar School. At that school I was in the 'house' named after him, I played rugby and cricket for 'Byron', and cheered on the athletes wearing the blue silk ribbon on Sports Day with a splendid illusion of taking part in something rather heroic. His lyric to Lochnagar ('Lachin Y Gair', 1807), for all its quality of a blurred and florid painting in oils, resonated for me because Lochnagar was for us *the* mountain: we walked up it from Glen Muick by Fox's Well, climbed its thousand-foot cliffs, and it was even visible from the city limits fifty miles away as a peaked rampart darkened by rainstorms, standing up like a blue banner striped with white, announcing summer.

The point of all this (apart from sheer self-indulgence) is to suggest what a heady multiple charge we got from the Highlands in their most local form, so much so that I have spent the years since trying to sort out what is valid and useful from the merely attitudinising. Byron's sense of mountainous wilderness was not all rhetoric. One crucial snatch of *Childe Harold* rings true, even though we may feel he has needed Wordsworth's help to say

> I live not in myself, but I become
> Portion of that around me; and to me,
> High mountains are a feeling, but the hum
> Of human cities torture: I can see
> Nothing to loathe in nature . . .[1]

Byron is here creating a *persona* very much of its time, a member of the same family as Rousseau, from the Swiss Alps, and Wordsworth, from the dales and fells of Cumberland.

7

Writers (mainly of the middle and upper classes) were now getting charges of energy and whole wells of material from beyond the pale – from the not-yet-colonised moors and mountains and deserts, and from the lives of peasants and hill-farmers, factory workers, the peoples of remote countries. A habit of identifying with the more turbulent and rough, the less genteel, biddable, schooled, or affluent, lies near the marrow of Romantic art during those years, from Blake's *Songs of Experience* and the storming of the Bastille at one end of the epoch to Delacroix's *Liberty on the Barricades* and the overthrow of the Bourbons in 1830: 'the definitive defeat of aristocratic by bourgeois power in western Europe', as it has been called, and 'the emergence of the working class as an open and self-conscious force'.[2]

Byron was born the year before the French Revolution and died the year the Combination Laws were repealed. Such were the events which challenged a person of that time to understand, to commit himself or not. Now, Byron was a vehement reviler of despots; 'king' for him was one of the dirtiest of words. His maiden speech in the House of Lords (on 27 February 1812) was against a Bill to make lawful the hanging of Luddites. One of the most sustained, least shallow or fitful passages in his poetry is the ten verses at the start of *Don Juan* Canto IX (1822), in which he analyses with implacably critical scorn the career of Wellington, great military hero and Prime-Minister-to-be. How deep did all this run in him? Was it from the centre of his poetic self? When he wrote most originally, how far was he drawing on social-radicalism, by which I mean solidarity with the forces making for change and against the ruling class?

Let us remind ourselves of the poetry concerned here. It consists of that page from *Don Juan* and many scathing asides from the same poem, for example on Castlereagh, the 'intellectual eunuch' –

> The vulgarest tool that tyranny could want,
> With just enough of talent, and no more,
> To lengthen fetters by another fix'd,
> And offer poison long already mix'd.[3]

Or on George IV –

> Gaunt Famine never shall approach the throne –
> Though Ireland starve, great George weighs twenty stone.[4]

These are epigrams, strung loosely on the picaresque tale. As such they belong with his other political two-liners, for example:

> So *He* has cut his throat at last. – *He? Who?*
> The Man who cut his Country's long ago.[5]

This is crunching stuff, and fearlessly outspoken, if you consider that it was aimed at a senior member of the Cabinet in an age when it had been made illegal to agitate against the monarchy and for a republic. True, it smacks of the squib, and specifically of a young man's naughty wish *pour épater les bourgeois*. He knew this himself, and when he wrote his 'Song for the Luddites' in the safety of Venice and sent it to Tom Moore, he lightlied it as 'an amiable *chanson* . . . I have written it principally to shock your neighbour . . . who is all clergy and loyalty'.[6] How far was Byron able to found a sustained poem on such materials, or rise to as convincing a political vision as Dryden's conservative ideal of 'solid Pow'r' in *Absalom and Achitophel*, say, or Pope's more liberal conception of enlightened landownership in his fourth *Moral Essay*? Twice, it seems to me, he nearly did, in *The Vision of Judgment* and *Don Juan* Canto IX, both written in 1822, at the juncture when the long and dreadful abeyance of libertarian politics under the war economy and the Gagging Acts was breaking out into the revolutionary ferment that produced the Reform Act of 1832.

At the start of *The Vision of Judgment*, before he has turned to his main business, which is the lampooning of the conformist Southey – his favourite butt and incarnation of mediocrity, as Shadwell was for Dryden or Dennis for Pope – Byron delivers himself of an impressively considered judgement on those last twenty-five years of George III's reign, which had seen the heyday of police spies, the hounding and parliamentary suppression of the early trade unions, and the frequent hanging of political prisoners:

In the first year of Freedom's second dawn
Died George the Third; although no tyrant, one
Who shielded tyrants, till each sense withdrawn
Left him nor mental nor external sun;
A better farmer ne'er brushed dew from lawn,
A worse king never left a realm undone!
He died – but left his subjects still behind,
One half as mad – and t'other no less blind.

A wonderfully black image is then created of the funerary
pomp, but it does not rest there: a traditional line of thought
about mortality is turned to insist on all the monarch has in
common with his subjects:

So mix his body with the dust! It might
Return to what it *must* far sooner, were
The natural compound left alone to fight
Its way back into earth, and fire, and air;
But the unnatural balsams merely blight
What Nature made him at his birth, as bare
As the mere million's base unmummied clay –
Yet all his spices but prolong decay.

This is a levelling wit, and the republicanism it implies is given
full voice when Satan makes his case for carrying King George
down to the nether world:

'Tis true, he was a tool from first to last
(I have the workmen safe); but as a tool
So let him be consumed . . .

'He ever warred with freedom and the free:
Nations as men, home subjects, foreign foes,
So that they utter'd the word "Liberty!"
Found George the Third their first opponent . . .

'The New World shook him off; the Old yet groans
Beneath what he and his prepared, if not
Completed: he leaves heirs on many thrones
To all his vices, without what begot
Compassion for him – his tame virtues; drones

> Who sleep, or despots who have now forgot
> A lesson which shall be re-taught them, wake
> Upon the throne of Earth; but let them quake![7]

The strength of this is not only in the idiomatic verve of the disparagements but also in the plain candour with which principles are invoked and tyranny confronted: 'he leaves heirs on many thrones'. To speak out so ringingly for republicanism was as bold, and personally as dangerous, as it has been in other places and times to declare for socialism or communism (or against Stalinism). For a generation it had been illegal 'to advocate the dethronement of the King, the establishment of a Republic, or the destruction of the Church,' or 'to organise bodies to achieve any or all of these things.' But by now, as a result of their hardships during the French Wars, the organised workers, for example the wool-combers and cotton-weavers, who had been 'Church and King' men, had declared for reform under a republic and Byron, in theory at least, was with them.[8]

This is also the tendency of that supreme passage in *Don Juan* Canto IX and the masterly poetry of it is sheerly Byronic, not in the best-seller sense of the word (the world-weary misanthrope cloaked and brooding in his exotic retreat), but in the aristocratic sophistication with which he turns and points and angles and inflects what at first seems to be a courtly tribute until it becomes an indictment:

> Oh, Wellington! (or 'Vilainton' – for Fame
> Sounds the heroic syllables both ways;
> France could not even conquer your great name,
> But punned it down to this facetious phrase –
> Beating or beaten she will laugh the same) . . .

Already the conservative reader might be feeling a little disconcerted as disrespect steals in on the heels of the honorific address. Within ten lines it is unmistakable:

> Though Britain owes (and pays you too) so much,
> Yet Europe doubtless owes you greatly more:
> You have repaired Legitimacy's crutch, –
> A prop not quite so certain as before:

> The Spanish, and the French, as well as Dutch,
>   Have seen, and felt, how strongly you *restore* . . .
>
> You are 'the best of cut-throats:' – do not start;
>   The phrase is Shakespeare's, and not misapplied: –
> War's a brain-spattering, windpipe-slitting art,
>   Unless her cause by Right be sanctified.
> If you have acted once a generous part,
>   The World, not the World's masters, will decide,
> And I shall be delighted to learn who,
>   Save you and yours, have gained by Waterloo?

So it unfolds, the apparently civil surface more and more roughened and darkened by cutting innuendoes, the formal address more and more loosened to let direct challenges break through:

> I am no flatterer – you've supped full of flattery:
>   They say you like it too – 'tis no great wonder:
> He whose whole life has been assault and battery,
>   At last may get a little tired of thunder . . .
> I've done. Now go and dine from off the plate
>   Presented by the Prince of the Brazils,
> And send the sentinel before your gate
>   A slice or two from your luxurious meals . . .
>
> I don't mean to reflect – a man so great as
>   You, my Lord Duke! is far above reflection . . .
> Though as an Irishman you love potatoes,
>   You need not take them under your direction;
> And half a million for your Sabine farm
> Is rather dear! – I'm sure I mean no harm.

The charade of courtesy and tribute has now played itself out: mention of past leaders (Epaminondas, Washington, Pitt) brings recent European history crunching in and the poem (virtually a self-contained anti-ode) raises itself to deliver an explicit and absolutely serious judgement:

> Never had mortal Man such opportunity,
>   Except Napoleon, or abused it more:
> You might have freed fall'n Europe from the Unity

Of Tyrants, and been blest from shore to shore:
And *now* – What *is* your fame? Shall the Muse tune it ye?
Now – that the rabble's first vain shouts are o'er?
Go, hear it in your famished Country's cries!
Behold the World! and curse your victories![9]

How supply Byron has toyed with his subject – how he has
entered demure disclaimers; promised to stop, then carried
on; appealed to virtues (while implying they are signally
missing); offered (impossible) advice with perfectly mimicked
mock-humility; kept his most pungent points for (apparently)
throw-away asides – until at last he draws himself up for that
clinching judgement. The passage is as fine as Mark Antony's
key speech in *Julius Caesar* (and twice as long) in its command
of speaking tone used right across the gamut, from trans-
parent insolence to naked challenge, and the subject it takes on
so frontally is the most powerful British person of the time, the
lynch-pin of its ruling class.

How disappointing it is, then, that the one movement of the
time with which Byron might have made common cause – the
Left Radicalism of Cobbett and Henry Hunt – found him
recoiling in a dislike which he overstates with the huffing-and-
puffing vehemence of any true-blue. In 1820 the Cato Street
conspiracy was unmasked. *Agents provocateurs* had pretended
that the Cabinet were to be together at a banquet and then
egged on a few desperate ultra-Radicals to plot their assassina-
tion. Secret policemen shopped them, five were hanged, and
their heads were held up for the London crowd to see –
'barricaded at a safe distance from the scaffold so that no
rescue could be attempted and no dying speeches heard.'[10]
They had planned, on a fairly fantastic plane, to seize the
arsenals, burn down the barracks, and set up a provisional
government in the Mansion House. But there was no rescue
attempt when the arrested men passed through London; the
leading Left Radicals, in the aftermath of the Peterloo Mas-
sacre, were studiously avoiding any rash provocations.[11] Yet
here is Byron's reaction to the affair, in a long political letter
sent from Ravenna to his closest friend in England, the MP
John Cam Hobhouse:

What a set of desperate fools these Utican Conspirators seem to have been. – As if in London after the disarming acts, or indeed at any time a secret could have been kept among thirty or forty. – And if they had killed poor Harrowby – in whose house I have been five hundred times – at dinners and parties – his wife is one of "the Exquisites" – and t'other fellows – what end would it have answered? – "They understand these things better in France" as Yorick says – but really if these sort of awkward butchers are to get the upper hand – *I* for one will declare *off*, I have always been (*before you* were – as you well know) a well-wisher to and voter for reform in Parliament – but "such fellows as these will never go to the Gallows with any credit" – such infamous Scoundrels as Hunt and Cobbett – in short the whole gang (always excepting you B. and D.) disgust and make one doubt of the virtue of any principle or politics which can be embraced by similar ragamuffins. – I know that revolutions are not to be made with rose-water, but though some blood may & must be shed on such occasions, there is no reasons it should be *clotted* – in short the Radicals seem to be no better than Jack Cade, or Wat Tyler – and to be dealt with accordingly.[12]

To take the measure of Byron's capitulation here to the merest reactionary panic, contrast the response of Cobbett himself to the labourers' revolt ten years later, when 'the fires were blazing, more or less, in SIXTEEN *of the counties of England*'. In the *Tuppenny Trash* for November 1830 he writes:

... our first feeling is that of *resentment against the parties*; but, when we have had a little time to reflect, we are, if we be not devourers of the fruit of the people's labours, led to ask, What can have been *the cause* of a state of things so unnatural as that in which crimes of this horrid sort are committed by hundreds of men going in a body, and deemed by them to be a sort of *duty* instead of *crimes*?

And in the *Political Register* for 4 December he answers his own question, ironically quoting

a great landholder, in Wiltshire, named BENNETT, who, upon being asked how much a labourer and his family ought *to have to live upon*, answered, "We calculate, that every

person in a labourer's family should have, *per week*, the price
of a gallon loaf, and three-pence over for *feeding* and
clothing, exclusive of house-rent, sickness, and casual expenses."

Mark! pray mark! a gallon loaf; that is to say, not quite *a
pound and a quarter of dry bread* and a *half-penny a day* for FOOD
and CLOTHING! And a SPECIAL COMMISSION is gone
into Wiltshire! There is a God of Justice, to be sure! That God
will do justice, in the end, to be sure! Talk of blasphemy,
indeed! Talk of Atheism! Who is not to be an Atheist, if he
believe there is no God to show displeasure at human
creatures (and those, too, who make all the food and all the
raiment to come) being doomed to exist on a pound and a
quarter of bread a day, and a half-penny for clothing, and
nothing for *drink*, and nothing for *fuel*, and nothing for
bedding, washing, or light![13]

Cobbett remembers the *grounds* of social revolt – hunger and
powerlessness (and carefully draws his evidence from a House
of Commons report). Byron does not, and treats the Radicals
as though they were just hooligans without a cause. To adapt
Paine on Burke, Byron scorns the plumage but he forgets the
dying bird. The Wellingtons of this world are fair game for racy
satire, but somehow this does not incline him to make
common cause with the tyrants' only effective opponents. A
few years before, he had refused to be panicked into reaction
by the revolt of the Luddites and had put his song into their
mouths:

> When the web that we weave is complete,
> And the shuttle exchanged for the sword,
>   We will fling the winding-sheet
>   O'er the despot at our feet,
> And dye it deep in the gore he has pour'd.[14]

A few years before that, in his speech to the House of Lords
against Lord Liverpool's bill to make frame-breaking a hanging offence, he had explicitly ridiculed scaremongering and
calls for heavyhanded policing: 'when at length the detach-
ments arrived at their destination in all "the pride, pomp and
circumstance of glorious war", they came just in time . . . to

collect the *spolia opima* in the fragments of broken frames, and return to their quarters amidst the derision of old women and the hooting of children'. He also spoke most feelingly about the men 'who never destroyed their looms till they were become useless', who were 'willing to dig, but the spade was in other hands', and who were 'famished into guilt' – a striking anticipation of the lines in the 'Internationale' about the 'criminals of want and prisoners of starvation'. And he affirmed the strength of the solidarity that held fast among the downtrodden workpeople: 'Those who refused to impeach their accomplices, when transportation was the only punishment, will hardly be tempted to witness against them when death is the penalty.'[15]

What had happened over the years to split Byron off from the popular movement? He defines part of the process himself, in a letter written during the epochal year of 1819:

You must not talk to me of England – that it is out of the question . . . Of the last, & best, ten years of my life, nearly six have been passed *out* of it – I feel no love for the soil after the treatment I received before leaving it for the last time – but I do not hate it enough to wish to take part in its calamities – as on either side harm must be done before good can accrue . . . My taste for revolution is abated – with my other passions.[16]

During those years of traumatic separation from his wife and daughter, Byron's main practical contact with England had consisted almost wholly of litigation to turn the coalfields he owned in Lancashire into ready money. He virtually owned Rochdale. He spent years trying to sell it. He was, in Cobbett's phrase, a 'devourer of the fruit of the people's labours', which fruit he spent on women, travel, and the Greek and Italian movements ('For three hundred pounds I can maintain in Greece... *rations* included, one hundred armed men *for three months!*': letter of 11 October 1823[17]).

My point here is in essence neither moral nor political, since the subject of this book is in the first place a poet. What I wish to account for is the oddly shallow-rooted and ephemeral nature of his *oeuvre*. He matured into very much a social-satirical sort of poet; the touchstones must therefore be

Langland and Chaucer, Dryden, Pope, and Burns. My view is, after repeated efforts over the years to winnow out a crop of substantial and permanently interesting poetry from all that rhetoric and all those beguiling tales, that Byron created remarkably few unforgettable and distinctive types – where, for example, is his Holy Willie or Sporus, his Achitophel or Wife of Bath? He is equally wanting in striking detail of social ritual, as opposed to stock theatrical gestures lightly sketched in; can one find in *Beppo* or *Don Juan*, say, many images of behaviour as distinct as Pope's 'Sir Plume, of amber snuff-box justly vain,/And the nice conduct of a clouded cane,' or Burns's louse 'struntin' rarely/Owre *gawze* and *lace*' on 'Miss's fine *Lunardi*'? In a short essay it is impossible to do more than sketch, or broach, the comparative judgement, but I suggest that if we want to recover the lineaments, the central institutions, and the typical denizens of particular societies – Lowland farm, kirk, and market town in Burns, say, or literary and political salons in Pope – we can derive a wealth of solid materials from those poets which is even historically useful because their focus is so sharp, their viewpoint so finely angled; whereas Byron (in Leavis's phrase) lacks 'constancy of point' and also density of knowledge. He is masterly at giving the feel of brilliant conversation (the spontaneous aside, the cavalier dismissal) but the gist is often desperately thin. And this is by no means a limitation of satire as such: in his own way Pope is wonderfully inward about the abortive struggles of the failed author in the passage from the *The Dunciad* which culminates in the image of 'Nonsense precipitate, like running Lead,/That slip'd thro' Cracks and Zig-zags of the Head,' and 'Holy Willie's Prayer' explores self-deceiving hypocrisy with the insight of a novelist.

The most usual way of accounting for this tendency of Byron's to deal superficially rather than profoundly with his materials would be in terms of personality: his painful awareness of being small, with a shortened leg, combined with his sophisticate's horror of being bored, led him to cover up sensitivity in a hardboiled manner and to debunk his deeper insights almost before they had been allowed to declare themselves. But this by itself is not enough, since a writer and his work are a psycho-social phenomenon and 'personality' is only psychological. I suggest that, to account for Byron, we have to see him as a Romantic Radical at a time when the Left movement in Britain was still raw and inchoate, prone to adventures, unable yet to create common cause between outstanding individuals and the mass of the people, deeply intimidated by the decades of Terror from 1797 to 1819, and not yet able to turn short-lived outrage (at Peterloo, for example) into a campaign with staying power (the Reform movement, the anti-Corn Law League, Chartism). In Scotland, the years of Byron's heyday have been characterised as 'a decade and a half of silence', during which troop movements and repressive policing 'quenched any flicker of revolutionary fire'.[18] In England it was the time of gagging acts and anti-combination laws, the terrorisation of the knitters and weavers who were losing their livelihoods to the new machines and the new shoddy goods, and a particularly discouraging, even dangerous time for writers: Blake belonged, with Tom Paine, to the Corresponding Society which supported democratic rights and the revolution in France; they were at risk of death if the police got on to them, and it may even be the case that Blake's dropping of his French Revolution poem in 1791, and the deflecting of his talents thereafter into huge diffuse allegories, was a forced flight from contemporary subject matter. This phase of literary history has been characterised as the 'period of the pseudo-romantics': a time of religious revival, traditionalism in taste (the ascendancy of Walter Scott), and a release of chauvinist emotion against the outright enemy, France.[19] The log-jam burst again: in England, in the post-war food riots and the first Hunger March; in Scotland, in the Radical War of 1819–20, in which weavers marched on the Carron armament factory, 60,000 workers downed tools for a week, and a call went out for a national strike. At once Byron was radicalised in his major poetry, as was Shelley, and we have the steeply-gathering wave represented by *The Vision of Judgment* plus the best of *Don Juan* and *The Age of Bronze*, Shelley's seven short poems of 1819 (before the 'West Wind' ode), *The Mask of Anarchy*, and *Peter Bell the Third*. As a 'school' of political poetry it was unprecedented and was not matched again until the

1960s; it also achieved a formidable unison. The full-throated judgmental voice Byron levelled at the nation's leaders just after 1820 was closely anticipated by Shelley's treatment of the Cabinet at the start of *The Mask of Anarchy*:

> Next came Fraud, and he had on,
> Like Eldon, an ermined gown;
> His big tears, for he wept well,
> Turned to mill-stones as they fell.

> And the little children, who
> Round his feet played to and fro,
> Thinking every tear a gem,
> Had their brains knocked out by them.[20]

Here is that same voice of barely-contained righteous scorn, gathered up into implacable accusation. Again, however, it is not sustained; the allegory of the *Mask*, after its biting specification of bishops, lawyers, peers, and spies, tails off into abstraction and fails to become a narrative. The fact is that both men were writing from a distance – from Italy. Both had been absent from Britain when the quickening undercurrents of revolution desperately needed spokesmen and rallying-points (and funds). Both, as a result, were lacking in a density of first-hand social materials such as would have been needed to nourish a major poetry and both, within a few years, were dead – avoidably, it could be said – the one kicking his heels in the malarial swamps of the Peloponnese while yearning for a soldier's part in the Greek wars of independence which was in fact closed to him, the other sailing a small boat into a storm in the Gulf of Spezia.

The two men's career's were remarkably alike: they were maverick aristocrats, people at a loss for function, tremendously eloquent in their attacks on the bugbears of the time – this king, that Secretary of State – but uncertain how to embody their sense of a better way or a way forward. E. H. Coleridge remarks that Byron was 'more of a king-hater than a people-lover. He was against the oppressors, but he despised and disliked the oppressed.'[21] Neither could come out with any positive value as rooted as Burns's

The Man's the gowd for a' that . . .

The pith o' Sense, and pride o' Worth,
Are higher rank than a' that,

which gives lyric force to fundamental egalitarian thoughts
uttered by Paine in *The Rights of Man* a few years before (for
example, France has 'put down the dwarf, to set up the man').
And both Shelley and Byron came out *against* the most
humane and honest politician of the time, and its most vivid
and informative writer, William Cobbett. In an epigram of 1820
Byron damns him to hell along with Paine.[22] In *Peter Bell the
Third*, written a few months after Peterloo, Shelley lumps
Cobbett with Castlereagh and Canning as one of the 'caitiff
corpses' who inhabit the contemporary inferno ('Hell is a city
much like London'), and then gets him quite wickedly wrong
in making out (as he also does in the swipe at 'vulgar agitators'
in his pamphlet on Reform) that Cobbett's politics were
vengeful or retributive:

Sometimes the poor are damned indeed
To take – not means for being blessed, –
But Cobbett's snuff, revenge; that weed
From which the worms that it doth feed
Squeeze less than they before possessed.[23]

Such ideas strike me as no more valid or thought-through than
the cant of the official spokesmen, in all countries, who try to
slight the outcry of the prisoners of starvation by smearing it as
a thing fomented by troublemakers from elsewhere.

To conclude by putting my argument dialectically: the
Radical movement in Scotland and England (as historians
have argued[24]) failed to find the leadership it needed, from
thinkers and poets among others, and the poets failed to
engage in the practical work, the engagement at close quarters
with native social experience, which might have saved them
from being what Arnold called 'beautiful and ineffectual
angels, beating their luminous wings in the void in vain'.
Furthermore, their more radical poems were alienated: they
were actually rejected or cast out by the society of their time.

John Murray would not publish *The Vision of Judgment* because Byron's *Cain* was being prosecuted and Longmans refused it because it might have spoiled the sales of Southey's encomium on the dead king. John Hunt published it and was prosecuted for his pains – as a result of which, in part, his brother Leigh withheld *The Mask of Anarchy* till 1832: it was thus denied any active role in the movement which had inspired it in the first place, and the rest of Shelley's poems in the revolutionary 1819 group stayed unpublished till 1839. Byron's Luddite song was unpublished until six years after his death. In the meantime a lotus-eating trance, a prolonged ascendancy of 'second-rate sensitive minds' (as Tennyson called himself), settled over literature. It was not replaced by something more talented and potent until Chartism and the Year of Revolutions in 1848 helped to engender the great age of realism in the novel.

NOTES

1. Byron, *The Complete Poetical Works*, ed. Jerome J. McGann (Oxford, 1980), II, 103.
2. E. J. Hobsbawm, *The Age of Revolution* (1962), 111.
3. *Poetical Works*, V, 7.
4. Ibid., 403.
5. *Byron's Letters and Journals*, ed. Leslie A. Marchand (1973–82), vol. 7, 210.
6. Ibid., vol.5, 149.
7. Byron *Works*, ed. E. H. Coleridge, (1901), IV, 489–91, 501–2.
8. G. D. H. Cole and Raymond Postgate, *The Common People* (1956 ed.), 181.
9. *Poetical Works*, V, 409–11.
10. E. P. Thompson, *The Making of the English Working Class* (1963), 705.
11. Ibid., 700.
12. *BLJ*, vol. 7, 62–3.
13. Quoted from *The Opinions of William Cobbett*, ed. G. D. H. and M. Cole (1944), 306, 308–9.
14. *Poetical Works*, IV, 48.
15. Quoted from A. L. Morton, *A People's History of England* (1948 ed.), 236; *A Handbook of Freedom*, ed. Jack Lindsay and Edgell Rickword (1939), 236–7.
16. *BLJ*, vol. 6, 226.

17. *Byron: A Self-portrait*, ed. Peter Quennell (1950), 752.
18. T. C. Smout, *A History of the Scottish People 1560–1830* (1972 ed.), 417.
19. Allan Rodway, *The Romantic Conflict* (1963), 13–22; the following wave he sees as a phase of 'unattained liberty' in which poets of 'European vision', Byron and Shelley, supplanted Wordsworth and Coleridge as the chief innovative talents.
20. Shelley, *The Complete Poetical Works*, ed. Thomas Hutchinson (Oxford, 1934), 338.
21. *Encyclopaedia Britannica* (1929), IV, 281.
22. *Poetical Works*, IV, 345.
23. *Poetical Works*, 350, 352; 'A Philosophical View of Reform': *Shelley's Prose*, ed. David Lee Clark (1988 ed.), 261.
24. Morton, *People's History of England*, 371.

Byron: Radical, Scottish Aristocrat

ANDREW NOBLE

The first generation of English Romantic poets was, initially, intensely radical. Whatever rejection or their aspirations followed, the young manhood of Wordsworth, Coleridge and Southey was in theory and, indeed, in self-endangering practice, committed to revolutionary change as the cause of the common people. Shelley and Byron, the aristocrats of the following generation, saw in their middle-class, middle-aged predecessors little but craven apostasy expressed in sycophantic, ambitious conduct. Southey, as Laureate, was the easiest target. Wordsworth, however, secreting himself in the decaying body of Lowther's aristocratic patronage, was almost equally heinous.

Neither Byron nor Shelley gave any credit to the fact that Wordsworth's conservatism was partly the result of direct experience of the Terror, with its manifestation of what Octavio Paz has defined as 'critical reason'.[1] More complex, however, is that Byron in particular seems not to have been aware that the prosody of Wordsworth's early, radical period and of his great poetry not only spoke of the suffering of the common people but, to a degree, employed the language of the common people. He shared Shelley's satirical sentiments, expressed in the latter's fine parody of Wordsworth, *Peter Bell the Third*, that Wordsworth's language was not only banal and pietistic but sententiously designed to make the people quiescent, rather than provoke them to action. As Shelley wrote of Peter Bell, standing as a servant in a demonic London behind Wordsworth's chair:

> And these obscure remembrances
> Stirred such harmony in Peter,
> That, whatsoever he should please,

23

He could speak of rocks and trees
In poetic metre.

For though it was without a sense
Of memory, yet he remembered well
Many a ditch and quick-set fence;
Of lakes he had intelligence,
He knew something of heath and fell.

He had also dim recollections
Of pedlars tramping on their rounds;
Milk-pans and pails; and odd collections
Of saws and proverbs; and reflections
Old parsons make in burying grounds.

But Peter's verse was clear, and came
Announcing from the frozen hearth
Of a cold age, that none might tame
The soul of that diviner flame
It augured to the Earth . . .[2]

Paul Foot has seen Shelley as such a divine, radical flame,
burning with a pure intensity in the people's cause.[3] In 1988
Michael Foot published *The Politics of Paradise: A Vindication of
Byron* in which he seeks to extend similar radical honours to
Byron. Certainly Byron, in his later poetry, displays a virile,
'flying', satirical destruction of the cant that glued together the
British establishment. A major part of Byron's enormous
poetic output is, however, neither of this quality nor nature.
Nor, though it might overwhelm a less credulous soul than
that of Michael Foot, is the splendid savaging of his apostate
elders irrefutable evidence as to the complete integrity of
Byron's own radicalism. Though Byron's Preface to *Don Juan*,
the companion piece to Shelley's *Peter Bell*, does display satiric
verve and analytic acumen it also, unintentionally, raises
difficult problems of Byron's language and prosody and,
hence, the authenticity of his politics:

The poem, or production, to which I allude, is that which
begins with – 'There is a thorn, it is so old' – and then the

Poet informs all who are willing to be informed, that its age was such as to leave great difficulty in the conception of its ever having been young at all – which is as much as to say, either that it was Coeval with the Creator of all things, or that it had been *born Old*, and was thus appropriately by antithesis devoted to the Commemoration of a child that died young. The pond near it is described, according to mensuration,

> 'I measured it from side to side:
> 'Tis three feet long, and two feet wide.'

Let me be excused from being particular in the detail of such things, as this is the Sort of writing which has superseded and degraded Pope in the eyes of the discerning British Public; and this Man is the kind of Poet, who, in the same manner that Joanna Southcote found many thousand people to take her to Dropsy for God Almighty re-impregnated, has found some hundreds of persons to misbelieve in his insanities, and hold him out as a kind of poetical Emanuel Swedenborg – a Richard Brothers, a Parson Tozer – half Enthusiast and half Imposter.

This rustic Gongora and vulgar Marini of his Country's taste has long abandoned a mind capable of better things to the production of such trash as may support the reveries which he would reduce into a System of prosaic raving, that is to supersede all that hitherto by the best and wisest of our fathers has been deemed poetry, and for his success – and what montebank will not find proselytes? (from Count Cagliostro to Madame Krudener) – he may partly thank his absurdity, and partly his having lent his more downright and unmeasured prose to the aid of a political party, which acknowledges its real weakness, though fenced with the whole armour of artificial Power, and defended by all the ingenuity of purchased Talent, in liberally rewarding with praise and pay even the meanest of its advocates. Amongst these last in self-degradation, this Thraso of poetry has long been a Gnatho in Politics, and may be met in print at some booksellers and several trunk-makers, and in person at dinner at Lord Lonsdale's.[4]

There is no little truth in this. Wordsworth's language can

descend from the prosaic to the disconcertingly banal. His
ultimate adherence to the Tory cause was politically dire and is
accurately reflected in the almost complete sterility of his late
poetry. Yet the early Wordsworth was not a decadent poet, the
betrayer of Pope's bequest. When radical in poetry and
politics, his plain speech had both borne historical witness to
the turbulence and sufferings of the age and brought into
human consciousness hitherto undiscerned states of memory
and being. If 'this Thraso of poetry has long been a Gnatho in
Politics' Hazlitt, perhaps echoing the phrase, pointed to an
anomaly in Byron at least as great. 'Lord Byron,' he wrote,
'who in his politics is a *liberal*, in his genius is haughty and
aristocratic.'[5]

Hazlitt perceived Byron as decadent aristocrat in both
politics and language. He had highly qualified opinions of
Pope's powers, and was less than impressed by Byron's
enthusiasm for him. For reasons we will later discuss, Hazlitt
was confused by the mock-heroics of Byron's great achievement, *Don Juan*. The tantrums of behaviour and language in
Byron's earlier poetic tales Hazlitt saw as largely vacuous and
self-indulgent. While Hazlitt could be as incisively bitter as
Byron about the apostate Wordsworth, he saw as the traitor to
poetry, poetry as the conserver of our common humanity, not
Wordsworth but Byron:

> I do not recollect, in all Lord Byron's writings, a single
> recurrence to a feeling or object that had ever excited an
> interest before; there is no display of natural affection – no
> twining of the heart round any object: all is the restless and
> disjointed affect of first impressions, or novelty, contrast,
> surprise, grotesque costume, or sullen grandeur. *His* beauties
> are the *houris* of Paradise, the favourites of a seraglio, the
> changing visions of a feverish dream. His poetry, it is true is
> stately and dazzling, arched like a rainbow, of bright and
> lovely hues, painted on the cloud of his own gloomy temper
> – perhaps to disappear as soon! It is easy to account for the
> antipathy between him and Mr Wordsworth. Mr Words-
> worth's poetical mistress is a Pamela; Lord Byron's an
> Eastern princess or a Moorish maid. It is the extrinsic, the
> uncommon that captivates him, and all the rest he holds in

sovereign contempt. This is the obvious result of pampered luxury and high born sentiments. The mind, like the palace in which it has been brought up, admits none but new and costly furniture. From a scorn of homely simplicity, and a surfeit of the artificial, it has but one resource left in exotic manners and preternatural effect. So we see in novels, written by ladies of quality, all the marvellous allurements of a fairy tale, jewels, quarries of diamonds, giants, magicians, condors and ogres. The author of the Lyrical Ballads described the lichen on the rock, the withered fern, with some peculiar feeling that he has about them: the author of Childe Harold describes the stately cypress, or the fallen column, with the feeling that every schoolboy has about them. The world is a grown schoolboy, and relishes the latter most.[6]

While Byron, in bad faith, might attack Wordsworth for finding 'some hundreds of persons to misbelieve in his insanities' so that he was 'half Enthusiast and half Imposter', it can be argued that imposture was of the essence of his own relationship to the hundreds of thousands who formed his credulous, immature audience. Hazlitt discerned that, paradoxically, it was Byron and his heroes' projection of aristocratic disdain which aroused mass enthusiasm and fed Byron's need to dominate his poetical contemporaries:

Whatever he does, he must do in a more decided and daring manner than anyone else – he lounges with extravagance, and yawns so as to alarm the reader! Self-will, passion, the love of singularity, a disdain of himself and of others (with a conscious sense that this is among the ways and means of procuring admiration) are the proper categories of his mind: he is a lordly writer, he is above his own reputation, and condescends to the Muses with a scornful grace![7]

Almost as seminal a literary sociologist as Coleridge, Hazlitt grasped that this was not merely regressive, *literary* excitement. It pointed in Byron's mass audience to an innate predisposition for aristocratic authority even, or indeed especially, in degenerate form. Byron as hero in life and letters was, if not a rebel in the cause of entrenched sycophancy, then at least the beneficiary of it:

Lord Byron complains that Horace Walpole was not properly appreciated, 'first, because he was a gentleman, and
secondly, because he was a nobleman.' His Lordship stands
in one, at least, of the predicaments here mentioned and yet
he has had justice, or somewhat more done to him. He
towers above his fellows by all the height of the peerage. If
the poet lends a grace to the nobleman, the nobleman pays it
back to the poet with interest. What a fine addition is ten
thousand a year and a title to the flaunting pretensions of a
modern rhapsodist! His name so accompanied becomes the
mouth well: it is repeated thousands of times, instead of
hundreds, because the reader in being familiar with the
Poet's work seems to claim acquaintance with the Lord.

'Let but a lord once own the happy lines:
How the wit brightens, and the style refines!'

He smiles at the high-flown praise or petty cavils of little
men. Does he make a slip in decorum, which Milton
declares to be the principal things? His proud crest and
armorial bearings support him: – no bend-sinister slurs his
poetical escutcheon! Is he dull, or does he put of some trashy
production on the public? Is it not charged to his account, as
a deficiency which he must make good at the peril of his
admirers. His Lordship is not answerable for the negligence
or extravagances of his Muse.[8]

Hazlitt found negligence and extravagance in abundance in
Byron's poetry. Without the dramatic objectivity and realism
of Walter Scott, far less of Shakespeare, with his unsurpassed
empathetic power, Byron's work was foetidly subjective to the
point of unreality. Hazlitt saw Byron, then, not as the inheritor
of eighteenth century satirical wit but as an aristocratic
vulgarian, who transmuted the golden rhetoric of the
seventeenth century into strident and sensational dross. His
poetry was the verbal equivalent of Beckford or Walpole's
Gothic architectural tastes, where historical forms reappeared
in unstable structures. Byron, for Hazlitt, was perpetually
shoring up his ruined poetic worlds with other men's fragments.

This may account for the charges of plagiarism which have

been repeatedly brought against the Noble Poet – if he can borrow an image or a sentiment from another, and heighten it by an epithet or allusion of greater force or beauty than is to be found in the original passage, he thinks he shows his superiority of execution in this in a more marked manner than if the first suggestion had been his own. It is not the value of the observation itself he is solicitous about; but he wishes to shine by contrast – even nature only serves as a foil to set off his style. He therefore takes the thoughts of others (whether contemporaries or not) out of their mouths, and is content to make them his own, to set his stamp upon them, by imparting to them a more meretricious gloss, a higher relief, a greater loftiness of tone, and a characteristic inveteracy of purpose.[9]

Edwin Muir has cogently argued that the secret of the Victorian bestseller's success was that the middle-brow audience could indulge and, indeed, endorse, their fantasies (erotic, martial, historical and exotic) in terms of literary allusiveness based on their still existent, if deteriorating, grasp of classic texts.[10] Their world was almost as densely intertextual as that of the post-modernist literary critic. If this is true, Byron is the progenitor of the nineteenth century bestseller. He certainly begat Disraeli.

The over-blown and sloppily second-hand defined by Hazlitt arguably derives from ethnic as well as social causes. Writing in 1937, in what is arguably still the finest contribution to an understanding of Byron's poetry, T. S. Eliot remarked that 'I therefore suggest considering Byron as a Scottish poet – I say "Scottish", not "Scots", since he wrote in English.'[11] Eliot's distinction is an important one, to which he returns. For the moment, however, let us not discuss the strengths which the Scottish tradition gave, albeit largely unconsciously, to Byron but the weaknesses so characteristic of the mainly unhappy history of the anglicisation of Scottish writing in the eighteenth and early nineteenth centuries. On the face of it they are a wildly mismatched couple, but as Eliot is subtly aware, there is considerable affinity between his own predicament and Byron's. Both were expatriates who aspired to manufacture a personality with which to advance themselves in their adopted land, and subsequently satirized that land in heroic-couplets. If for Eliot *Don Juan* marked the success of Byron's satire, it was a splendid summit resting atop a disconcerting mountain of verbiage:

> Of Byron one can say, as of no other English poet of his eminence, that he added nothing to the language, that he discovered nothing in the sounds, and developed nothing in the meaning of individual words. I cannot think of any other poet of his distinction who might so easily have been an accomplished foreigner writing English. The ordinary person talks English, but only a few people in every generation can write it; and upon this undeliberate collaboration between a great many people talking a living language and a very few people writing it, the continuance and maintenance of a language depends. Just as an artisan who can talk English beautifully while about his work or in a public bar, may compose a letter painfully written in a dead language bearing some resemblance to a newspaper leader, and decorated with words like 'maelstrom' and 'pandemonium': so does Byron write a dead or dying language.[12]

Unlike Hazlitt, Eliot thought Byron's true weakness lay not in platitudinous schoolboy thought but in his 'schoolboy command' of the language. He compared Byron's treatment of Waterloo unfavourably to Stendhal's in its lack of 'minute particulars' but, disconcertingly, felt that poetic good had been achieved in this stanza from *Childe Harold*:

> And wild and high the 'Cameron's gathering' rose!
> The war-note of Lochiel, which Albyn's hills
> Have heard, and heard, too, have her Saxon foes; –
> How in the noon of night that pibroch thrills,
> Savage and shrill! But with the breath which fills
> Their mountain-pipe, so fill the mountaineers
> With the fierce native daring which instils
> The stirring memory of a thousand years,
> And Evan's, Donald's fame rings in each clansman's ears![13]

This spirited burst, Eliot believed, came from his 'mother's people'. It seems rather to have come from Walter Scott, whom

Byron displaced as the best-selling narrative poet of the age and whose enormous prestige and commercial success was in major part due to his rendition of 'romantic' Scottish themes.

The Enlightenment manifested itself in Scotland principally in an extraordinary evolution of economics, the social sciences, mental philosophy of a sceptical toughness and technology. Simultaneously, Scotland, due to the accident of Highland geography and history, became the favoured location for the fantasies of educated nineteenth-century man. Overtly given to progress, European man was suffused with a profound nostalgia for the world he was leaving, indeed often destroying, and so much of eighteenth century bestselling writings are compensatory fantasies for this passing world. James MacPherson was the primary, knowing benefactor of these appetites for the militaristic, the melancholic, for feudal and aristocratic trappings, all tinged with the fey and supernatural. Scott perfected this by creating forms which permitted fantasy, yet assured the bourgeois reader of the ultimate success and security-of his ordered, respectable commercial world. There may be a law which states that bad literature abhors a partial national vacuum and rushes in to fill it. In part a synthetic, literary personality, Byron derived his fiscally rewarding insubstantiality from the synthetic Scottishness apparent in his early reworkings of Ossian and other Highland themes.

The principal cause of Scott's enormous literary and commercial success was his sensational variations on a theme wherein a martial insurrectionary hero of primitive, feudal energies *temporarily* endangers an increasingly prosperous, homogenizing commercial society. Thus, the failed Jacobite threat to the Union created a perfect historical paradigm for his fictions. Less obvious was the fact that Scott was more concerned with the Jacobins than the Jacobites. Even the sceptical Hazlitt did not read in Scott's fiction the conservative elements he discovered in his personality. Hazlitt, in fact, provides perhaps unsurpassed testimony to the power Scott's rebarbative fantasies had for prudent, rational man in the early nineteenth century:

Protestants and Papists do not now burn one another at the

stake: but we subscribe to new editions of *Fox's Book of Martyrs*; and the secret of the success of the *Scotch Novels* is much the same – they carry us back to the feuds, the heart-burnings, the havoc, the dismay, the wrongs and the revenge of a barbarous age and people – to the rooted prejudices and deadly animosities of sects and parties in politics and religion, and of contending chiefs and clans in war and intrigue. We feel the full force of the spirit of hatred with all of them in turn. As we read, we throw aside the trammels of civilisation, the flimsy veil of humanity. 'Off, you lendings!' The wild beast resumes its sway within us, we feel like hunting-animals, and as the hound starts in his sleep and rushes on the chase in fancy, the heart rouses itself in its native lair, and utters a wild cry of joy, at being restored once more to freedom and lawless, unrestrained impulses. Every one has his full swing, or goes to the Devil in his own way. Here are not Jeremy Bentham's Panopticons, none of Mr Owen's impassable Parallelograms, (Rob Roy would have spurned and poured a thousand curses on them), no long calculations of self-interest – the will takes its instant way to its object; as the mountain-torrent flings itself over the precipice, the greatest possible good of each individual consists in doing all the mischief he can to his neighbour: that is charming, and finds a sure and sympathetic chord in every breast! So Mr Irving, the celebrated preacher, has rekindled the old, original, almost exploded hell-fire in the aisles of the Caledonian Chapel, as they introduce the real water of the New River at Sadler's Wells, to the delight and astonishment of his fair audience. *'Tis pretty, though a plague,* to sit and peep into the pit of Tophet, to play at *snap-dragon* with flames and brimstone (it gives a smart electrical shock, a lively fillip to delicate constitutions), and to see Mr Irving, like a huge Titan, looking as grim and swarthy as if he had to forge tortures for all the damned![14]

The last thing, of course, that Scott wanted was a phenomenon anything akin to Rob Roy let loose in contemporary society. Byron's eruption on the scene caused him, consequently, far more alarm than the loss of his role as the age's chief narrative poet. His fictional success was more than adequate consolation for that. What did alarm him was that Byron, as Napoleon, appeared unholily like a terrible dream made flesh; that a rough, slouching beast had, indeed, been born. Scott saw on Byron and his associate of his early European travels, John Hobhouse, distinct marks of the revolutionary beast. As Malcolm Kelsall has noted:

> Scott categorized Hobhouse's commentary as a 'frenzy' improper to 'individuals of birth and education' (patricians), and Byron and his commentator showed that they were 'trained in the school of revolutionary France' (Jacobins). It ill became Byron to complain of British liberty when it was only as a result of the freedom which Britain has won that the poet might visit Europe (thus Scott is directly in the tradition of Addison's *Letter from Italy*).[15]

Scott was suffused with desire to fill his own life with all the trappings of aristocracy. Hence Hazlitt's acerbic aside that 'Sir Walter Scott (when all's said and done) is an inspired butler.' Consequently, Scott found Byron's treachery to his own class incomprehensible. In discussing Canto IV of *Childe Harold*, Scott saw the threat to social order and relative prosperity of the new individualism personified in Byron:

> This moral truth appears to us to afford, in great measure, a key to the peculiar tone of Lord Byron. How then, will the reader ask, is our proposition to be reconciled to that which preceded it? If the necessary result of an enquiry into our own thoughts be the conviction that all is vanity and vexation of spirit, why should we object to a style of writing, whatever its consequences may be, which involves in it truths as certain as they are melancholy? If the study of our own enjoyments leads us to doubt the reality of all except the indisputable pleasures of sense, and inclines us therefore towards the Epicurean system – it is nature, it may be said, and not the poet which urges us upon the fatal conclusion. But this is not so. Nature, when she created man a social being, gave him the capacity of drawing that happiness from his relations with the rest of the race, which he is doomed to seek in vain in his own bosom. These relations cannot be the source of happiness to us if we despise or hate the kind with whom it is their office to unite

us more closely. If the earth be a den of fools and knaves, from whom the man of genius differs by the more mercurial and exalted character of his intellect, it is natural that he should look down with pitiless scorn on creatures so inferior. But if, as we believe, each man, in his own degreee, possesses a portion of the ethereal flame, however smothered by unfavourable circumstances, it is or should be enough to secure the most mean from the scorn of genius as well as from the oppression of power, and such being the case, the relations which we hold with society through all their graduations are channels through which the better affections of the loftiest may, without degradation, extend themselves to the lowest. Farther, it is not only our social connections which are assigned to us in order to qualify that contempt of mankind, which too deeply indulged tends only to intense selfishness; we have other and higher motives for enduring the lot of humanity – sorrow, and pain, and trouble – with patience of our own griefs and commiseration for those of others.[16]

As with a host of other contemporary phenomena, there seems good cause to believe that Scott vastly overestimated the revolutionary potential present in Byron. It took Dostoevsky in *The Possessed* to see how aristocratic *ennui* might become the medium through which psychotic revolutionary violence could discharge itself. Marilyn Butler is much more accurate in discerning the manner in which the Byronic here did not invert Scott's morality but, in fact, subtly reinforced it.

Byron now succeeded Scott as the most fashionable author of the day, and he did not because his appeal, which was superficially rebellious and hence exciting, remained at a deeper level bi-partisan. In *Childe Harold*, *The Giaour*, *The Bride of Abydos*, *The Corsair* and *Lara* he developed the Byronic hero from prototypes such as Schiller's Karl Moor and Scott's Marmion. Masterful, moody outlaws, haunted by some secret consciousness of guilt, these heroes act as a focus for contemporary fantasies. Not the least element of guilty complicity about them is that they echo the French cult of Napoleon: they are fictional equivalents of Géricault's handsome idealized portrait of the French emperor on a white charger surmounting the Alps. By this daring hint, and by translating his hero from Scott's historical setting to a present-day theatre of war, Byron implies the possibility of effective action in the real world. Even so, his rebellious Corsair is sanitized, as far as the English public is concerned, by wielding his sword well away from the French proponents of liberty and equality, and still further from the machine-breakers and petitioners of the English provinces. Nor has his rebellion any hint of a philosophic dimension. It is drained of ideological content, to a degree actually remarkable in the literature of the period. An image potentially of revolution is presented in terms sufficiently unintellectual to allay the fears of the propertied public.[17]

The collusion between Byron and his propertied audience is perhaps even more subtle. Byron purveyed melodramatically the moody-browed man of will, a cardboard cut-out of Hegel's world spirit. This figure, however, was already beyond action, in a state of vacuity and emotional paralysis. Perhaps a celebrant of a love that did not dare speak its name, he was certainly a possessor of a guilt that refused to define its nature and origin. In a brilliant new essay, 'What's Eating Lara?', Dan Jacobson notes that on this core issue of unrevealed guilt Byron 'like any other bad writer, is trying to get out of the reader (amazement, fear, admiration) on tick, as it were – without delivering the goods.' Jacobson continues:

It is not just that the readers of Byron's age, like readers today, enjoyed trash; and the more portentious it was, the more fluent, the more titillatingly knowledgeable about evil, the more 'literary' in certain obvious ways, the more they admired it. (Again, just like readers today – though the styles of vulgarity we respond to are different.) There is another and more interesting sense in which one can account for their success. What made them so effective in reaching into the minds of their readers is that they are *about* hollowness, they are about bad faith and insincerity. Indeed one can go further and say that the central tormenting secret which the heroes of the poems (and their creator) try to guard so jealously from prying eyes is their own suspicion that they are fakers.[18]

For Jacobson, Byron's poetry, other than *Don Juan* with its comic, multi-voiced scepticism, is to be read as revealing or, indeed, betraying the reverse of its intentions:

His narrative poems, with that fixed demonic scowl on their foreheads, were the literary record of his attempt to overcome by an effort of will what I have called the torment of insincerity which had always haunted him. Every clenched denial and fierce assertation in these poems, every dark hint of what had better been left unspoken, had been intended to silence not only the doubters and deriders without – though on the whole they had shown themselves only too eager to be convinced – but the many sceptical voices within.[19]

The true revolutionary, for good or ill, is by definition a man of sincerity; for him desire and action are wholly congruent. In a recent book, *Byron's Politics*, Malcolm Kelsall explains Byron's vacuity and near paralysis of political will, despite his manifest political involvement in the Lords and elsewhere, as stemming from his belonging to a Whig tradition and establishment that had not only lost power but could not foresee its restitution. Kelsall very successfully repudiates the concept of Byron's 'iron revolutionary will' by demonstrating the relationship between his private correspondence and his dramatization of the dilemma faced by both himself and his party. From the outset, of course, Whig radicalism had always been brought up short when the claims of social citizenship infringed on the rights of property. Byron, the Nottinghamshire mine-owner, was actually aware of this predicament:

I look upon [convulsion] as inevitable, though not revolutionist: I wish to see the English constitution restored, and not destroyed. Born an aristocrat, and naturally one by temper, with the greater part of my property in the funds, what have *I* to gain by a revolution?[20]

If revolution for the Whigs was to stop well short of redistribution of property, taking arms with the people was also far beyond the pale. Peterloo and Cato Street evoked in him responses akin to the more comprehensible paranoia present in Scott.

The reverse of the Byron, who at a safe distance from England donned the garb of a revolutionary leader in Italy and

Albania and Greece, and who saw such a leadership as a pure manifestation of the radical, nationalist popular will, this native Byron saw in revolution at home merely the manipulation of the common people by psychotic demagogues:

I am convinced – that Robespierre was a Child – and Marat a quaker in comparison of what they would be [Hunt and Cobbett] could they throttle their way to power.

I can understand and enter into the feelings of Mirabeau and La Fayette – but I have no sympathy with Robespierre – and Marat – whom I look upon as in no respect worse than those two English ruffians.[21]

Kelsall shows cogently how this moral dilemma, a product of the practical impotence and theoretical confusion of Whig politicians, runs through Byron's work. *Marino Falierio*, a bad play showing, as so often, Byron's lack of proper anxiety concerning Shakespeare's influence, is however perhaps the purest paradigm of this dilemma. Historical Venice, a 'sea-Sodom', mirrors the decay Byron felt present in another naval empire, contemporary England. Falierio, the Doge cannot bring himself to make common cause with the people against his peers, and cleanse the corruption of the state in a bloody flux of aristocratic blood. It is Falierio himself who ends in melodramatic execution. Hazlitt, eager for the overthrow of a corrupt establishment, liked the play's artistry little and its dramatization of vacillating politics even less.[22]

If, as Kelsall suggests, Byron was rendered impotent as a revolutionary by his bonds of birth and ideology to the Whig élitist cause, it is also true that this problem of class was intensified by his Scottishness. The revolutionary period into which Byron entered was not only that of republicanism but of nationalism; it was the age of the birth and rebirth of nations. In his excellent *The Break-up of Britain*, Tom Nairn has pointed to the peculiar paradox that in an age of national revolutions and heightened national consciousness throughout Europe, Scotland, peculiarly, intensified its links with England. Nairn cogently argues that we can account for this paradox because, uncharacteristic of other national movements, the Scottish élite had been so advantageously educated in the eighteenth century that they did not form an alienated group when

revolution broke in America and France, and were commer-
cially and professionally integrated into British society to a
degree that a commitment to a Scottish cause would have
seemed socially and fiscally self-endangering. The dispos-
sessed Burns was certainly fired by General Washington and
events in France, but his exception proves Nairn's rule. Sir
James MacIntosh in *Vindice Gallicae* did envisage the importa-
tion of Scotland's awareness of its historical roots, but this was
an idea which found little favour among his peers and one
which he himself was soon to deny. Sir Walter Scott, notor-
iously for Hugh MacDiarmid and other modern nationalist
intellectuals, solved the problem by creating massive enthusiasm for inessential, 'romantic' symbols of Scottish nationalism while in reality being terrified of the resurrection of what
he considered a rebarbative Scotland, and consequently pas-
sionately committed himself to social and economic salvation
through the Union. These lines, however, are not by the
pro-Unionist, Tory Scott but the allegedly radical Byron:

> Who hath not glowed above the page where Fame
> Hath fixed High Caledon's unconquered name;
> The mountain-land which spurned the Roman chain,
> And baffled back the fiery-crested Dane,
> Whose bright claymore and hardihood of hand
> No foe could tame – no tyrant could command?
> That race is gone – but still their children breathe,
> And Glory crowns them with redoubled wreath:
> O'er Gael and Saxon mingling banners shine,
> And England! add their stubborn strength to thine.
> The blood which flowed with Wallace flows as free,
> But now 'tis only shed for Fame and thee![23]

It was not the least of the successes of the imperial enterprise:
to convert their most feared eighteenth-century adversaries
into the sharpest cutting edge of its nineteenth century
overseas conquests. It is extraordinary to find Byron lending
his name to the cause. It is absurd when we consider that in
Italy, Albania and Greece he lent his name, money and
energies to succouring European national movements not his
own. A similar pattern can be observed in Boswell earlier and

R. L. Stevenson later. Such Scottish writers seem to be subconsciously driven into a displaced nationalism, which asserts its inauthenticity by degenerating into a kind of costume melodrama. Byron's theatricality had a source in an even less likely element of his Scottishness. Byron, Edwin Muir has remarked, 'appeared assiduously in society as an *âme damnée*'.[24] Given its long history of sermonising monologues against the dialectical nature of the theatre, it is no little irony that by the late eighteenth century, Scottish Calvinism appears in theatrical form in British culture's burgeoning Gothic sensibility. While it never had the obsessive force of Italian Roman Catholicism, with its orgiastic fantasies polluted by sadistic monks and erotic nuns, Scottish Calvinism did breathe sexually titillating tongues of fire. Hazlitt has a marvellous, comic description of London's Caledonian Chapel with the Rev Edward Irving as celeberity preacher at that unfallen stage in his career when Christ's sexual nature was still only a matter of rhetoric.[25]

A major part of Byron's appeal, his ability to 'express before anybody else what a great number of people wanted to have expressed for them', seems to have stemmed from his capacity to appear as simultaneously the rebel against and victim of sexually repressive religion.[26] It is, of course, of the nature of radical politics to see in unexploited sexuality an essential element of the democratic freedom it seeks. Byron follows on the heels of William Blake and Mary Wollstonecraft. Yet the cleansing purity of Blake's vision seems quite lost in Byron. At worst he seems to have made himself master of ceremonies for the children of the middle-classes to indulge in promiscuity in the name of liberty – as in the 1960's – and subsequently retreat back into comfortable conformity. We also feel that Byron's constant posing as 'something demonic rather than human, a Miltonic Satan or fallen angel' is not like Blake's radical transvaluation of values but a kind of theatricality. I have argued elsewhere, comparing Blake with Burns, that we can perceive a similar self-dramatising demonism in Burns who, like Byron, often referred to his sibling relationship to Milton's Satan.[27] These Scottish poets, at the end of the day, always imply that their manic rebellion will end, like Milton's Satan, in depressed defeat at the hands of institutional authority. It lends veracity to these sentiments that this is how Burns and Byron did end. Calvinism, at least as late as Stevenson, seems to have politically unmanned the Scottish creative writer. Since terrible paternal authority can be attacked but never overcome, as in Boswell, erotic or political radicalism will inevitably end in punishment and defeat. Byron, another archetypal Scottish Calvinist writer, was, therefore, by inheritance flawed at the heart of his radical will. The melodramatic, intense, brooding wilfulness of his heroes, as Jacobson has suggested, masked an underlying chaos of conflicting emotions. Or, as Edwin Muir has remarked:

> He preferred to paint this weak good-nature as something very like villainy, and thought it better to be thought wicked than feeble-willed. The fatal complications in which he involved himself during the five years of public success in London might as readily have been brought about by weakness as by double-dyed infamy; and indeed, seen through Byron's predestinarian spectacles, the one became indistinguishable from the other.[28]

Though Hazlitt has many profound and painful things to say about Scotsmen and what religious repression did to them, he never seems to have penetrated beneath Byron's aristocratic surface to the tumult within and out of which the late poetry developed. This led him to misunderstand the quintessentially Scottish achievement of *Don Juan*. Ironically, Hazlitt defined arguably the central characteristic of authentic Scottish poetry without being able to appreciate it.

> The *Don Juan* indeed has great power; but its power is owing to the force of the serious writing, and to the oddity of the contrast between that and the flashy passages with which it is interlarded. From the sublime to the ridiculous there is but one step. You laugh and are surprised that any one should turn around and *travestie* himself: the drollery is in the utter discontinuity of ideas and feelings. He makes virtue serve as a foil to vice; *dandyism* is (for want of any other) a variety of genius. A classical intoxication is followed by the splashing of soda-water, by frothy effusions of ordinary bile. After the lightning and the hurricane, we are introduced to the

interior of the cabin and the contents of wash-hand basins. The solemn hero of tragedy plays *Scrub* in the farce. This is 'very tolerable and not to be endured.' The Noble Lord is almost the only writer who has prostituted his talents in this way. He hallows in order to desecrate; takes a pleasure in defacing the images of beauty his hands have wrought; and raises our hopes and our belief in goodness to Heaven only to dash them to earth again, and break them in pieces the more effectually from the very height they have fallen. Our enthusiasm for genius or virtue is thus turned into a jest by the very person who has kindled it, and who thus fatally quenches the sparks of both.[29]

Adherents of MacDiarmid will have observed that what Hazlitt here negates, the Scottish poet sees as the quintessential, creative zig-zag of Scottish poetry with its dynamic interaction of disparate elements.[30] Eliot also recognised this in Byron and sensed a 'flyting' satirical tone in *Don Juan* that he traced back to Dunbar. Eliot also recognised in the achievement of Byron's last, great mock epic a 'left-field', rapscallion element that MacDiarmid would have applauded as the true voice of Scottish poetry. Hazlitt forgave Byron much for the manner of his death. The mass of bad poetry, inflaming rather than purging his audience's doubtful social passions, can be equally forgotten in the face of his last poem, whose achievement Eliot so cogently defines:

I do not pretend that Byron is Villon (nor, for other reasons, does Dunbar or Burns equal the French poet), but I have come to find in him certain qualities, besides his abundance, that are too uncommon in English poetry, as well as the absence of some vices that are too common. And his own vices seem to have twin virtues that closely resemble them. With his charlatanism, he has also an unusual frankness; with his pose, he is also a *poète contumace* in a solemn country; with his humbug and self-deception he has also a reckless raffish honesty; he is at once a vulgar patrician and a dignified toss-pot; with all his bogus diabolism and his vanity of pretending to disreputability, he is genuinely superstitious and disreputable. I am speaking of the qualities and defects visible in his work, and important in estimating his work: not of the private life, with which I am not concerned.[31]

NOTES

1. See that incomparable contemporary poet-critic's *Children of the Mire: Modern Poetry from Romanticism to the Avant-Garde* (1974).
2. *The Complete Poetical Works of Percy Bysshe Shelley*, ed. Hutchinson (1956), Part the Fifth, stanzas x–xiii, 355–6.
3. *Red Shelley* (1980).
4. *Byron's 'Don Juan'*, ed. Steffen and Pratt (1957), II, 3–4.
5. 'Lord Byron', *Collected Writings*, ed. P. P. Howe (1932), vol. 11, 70–1.
6. 'Byron and Wordsworth', *Collected Writings*, vol. 20, 155–6.
7. 'Lord Byron', 70.
8. 'On the Aristocracy of Letters', *Collected Writings*, vol. 8, 209–10.
9. 'Lord Byron', 70.
10. 'Best Sellers of Yesterday: VI William Black', *Edwin Muir: Uncollected Scottish Criticism*, ed. Noble (1982), 222–7.
11. 'Byron' in *English Romantic Poets*, ed. M. H. Abrams (1960), 197.
12. Ibid., 203–4.
13. *Complete Poetical Works*, ed. J. J. McGann, vol. II, Canto the Third, Stanza 26.
14. 'On the Pleasure of Hating', *Collected Writings*, vol. 12, 129.
15. *Byron's Politics* (1987), 77.
16. *Miscellaneous Prose Works*, vol. XVII (1843), 359–60.
17. *Romantics, Rebels and Reactionaries* (1981), 118–19. We should probably read David for Géricault here.
18. *Adult Pleasures* (1988), 35.
19. Ibid., 37.
20. Quoted by Kelsall, 83.
21. Ibid., 86.
22. 'Lord Byron's *Tragedy of Marino Faliero*', *Collected Writings*, vol. 19, 44–51.
23. 'Address Intended to be Recited at the Caledonian Meeting', *Complete Poetical Works* (1981), vol. III, 270–1.
24. 'A Romantic Poet', *Edwin Muir: Uncollected Scottish Criticism*, 206.
25. 'Pulpit Oratory – Dr Chalmers and Mr Irving', *Collected Writings*, vol. 20, 113–22.
26. Both Eliot and Muir have accurate analyses of this ambivalence in Byron.
27. 'Burns, Blake and Romantic Revolt' in *The Art of Robert Burns*, eds. Jack and Noble (1982), 191–214.
28. 'A Romantic Poet', 207.
29. 'Lord Byron', *Collected Writings*, vol. 11, 75.

30. 'This Scottish strain is tremendously idiosyncratic, full of a wild humour which blends the actual and the apocalyptic in an incalculable fashion.' *Albyn or Scotland and the Future* (1927), 22.
31. 'Byron', 209.

Byron and Catholicism

WILLIAM J. DONNELLY

Byron, in his letters, said a considerable amount about Catholicism, particularly during his years of exile in southern Europe. I would admit that we cannot make too much of this material, which is qualified by the occasional flippancy of tone. Moreover, elsewhere in Byron's writings there are many more negative references to religion in general. Nevertheless, I have sought to place his remarks on Catholicism in the context both of Byron's Romanticism and his Scottish background.

First of all then, in speaking about religion, it can be argued that we are concerned with what is, in the widest sense, the central feature of Romantic poetry, reacting as it does against the emphasis on science and rationalism which had begun with the Renaissance and reached its zenith during the Age of Enlightenment in the eighteenth century. Collectively, Byron's fellow Romantic poets reject as inadequate a view of life based solely on science and reason and seek a more satisfactory definition of existence with reference beyond such terms. In so doing, they might all be deemed religious, in the broadest sense of the term. Thus, when Blake seeks 'To see a World in a Grain of Sand/And Heaven in a Wild Flower' he is essentially religious, in that reason sees a grain of sand in a grain of sand, while to science, a wild flower is a botanical specimen. In the same way, the epigraph at the beginning of Coleridge's *Ancient Mariner* declares the need to:

. . . contemplate in my mind the idea of a greater and better world, lest the mind, grown used to dealing with small matters of everyday life should dwindle, and become wholly submerged in petty thoughts.[1]

In the poem itself, as in most of Coleridge's poetry, he seeks to put this into practice. That is, he seeks to express a consciousness of a world beyond that of material reality. The title of

Wordsworth's famous ode 'Intimations of Immortality from Recollections of Early Childhood' speaks for itself in this regard, and again it could be said to indicate his central concern in much of his major work. Even Keats, who rejects Christianity, is nevertheless obsessed in his poetry by the sad inadequacy of this mortal world, and tantalised by the vision, or the illusion, of an immortal solution. The odes to Psyche, to the Nightingale, to the Grecian Urn, for example, are all images of this. Finally Shelley, though militantly atheist, is concerned to condemn as inadequate a purely rationalist view of existence, and to assert instead the primacy of that which is beyond reason, that is the imagination, and the vision of human perfectibility which the imagination can envisage.

What then of Byron? In the light of all this, Byron is distinct and unique among Romantic poets in having little or no time for religious or visionary solutions to the human predicament. While he deeply abhors the sad reality of the human lot, he proposes no transcendental compensations. On the other hand, while with Shelley he feels the need to defy and resist tyranny at all cost, he does not really have any faith in Shelley's view of a perfectible world. His view of the human condition is summed up in the figure of the notorious Byronic hero – of Cain, of Manfred, of Childe Harold, among others – a hero defiant but damned, an outcast in this world, and in any other.

Now on several occasions Byron's distinct and unique viewpoint has been attributed to the influence of his Scottish Calvinist background. Angus Calder, for example, has recently written of the poet's 'secular Calivinism',[2] secular, in that he is no transcendentalist, yet Calvinist, in that he sees no salvation in another world, or in this one. I should like to suggest my understanding of the source of this condition, in that it may shed some light on our later discussion of Byron's response to Catholicism.

What does Byron himself say about his Calvinist background? While for the most part he gloried in his Scottish upbringing, his references to its Calvinist aspect are all negative – I should say that we are speaking here of the dogma that Burns satirised so brilliantly, which has nothing to do with Presbyterianism as we know it, which in many respects presents quite the opposite religious view. Thus he speaks of '. . . being early disgusted with a Calvinistic Scotch school where I was cudgelled to Church for the first ten years of my life.'[3] And again, 'I was bred in Scotland among Calvinists in the first part of my life – which gave me a dislike of that persuasion . . .'[4] However, perhaps more important than Byron's reaction to Calvinist religion was the effect upon him of the psychological ambience that Calvinism created, by which he would inevitably have been influenced.

Essentially, the pre-Reformation Church was, rightly or wrongly, a vehicle whereby the inescapable imperfection of the human being could be catered for. Paintings, statues, rituals, sacraments, and most obviously the sacrament of Penance, were all sources of intercession, mediation, reconciliation. By contrast, and again rightly or wrongly, post-Reformation Calvinism was an absolute denial of this function, with profound psychological implications. Such a denial leaves the imperfect individual, and imperfect humanity at large, uncatered for, unreconciled, irredeemable – but for those arbitrarily elected to salvation through the doctrine of predestination.

To such a terrible psychological burden there seem to be two notable responses. The one is honest while the other is dishonest, but perhaps understandable in the circumstances. The second of these is to deem oneself elected to salvation in a world in which most of one's fellows are hopelessly damned. The double standards which this mental shuffle necessitates has of course provided a rich seam for the Scottish writer, being the basis of Burns's kirk satires, Hogg's *Justified Sinner* and several works by Stevenson as well as the most obvious, *Jekyll and Hyde*, to go no further. It may well be the source of Byron's oft-repeated detestation of cant.

Alternatively, the honest response to the situation would be to conclude that our unreconciled imperfections must indeed render us irredeemable, that there is no solution to our predicament in this world or in any other: we can either despair, or defy. It might be argued then that the defiant, damned Byronic hero becomes more fully comprehensible in the context of this psychological ambience created by Calvinism. While rejecting the Calvinist religion, he remains a 'secular Calvinist', and therefore his is a vision of unaccommodated man, in every sense of the term. Perhaps in the light of this peculiarly Scottish Romanticism, we can give some shape to Byron's responses to Catholicism.

It should be noted that, in a Britain remaining fairly hostile to Catholicism, Byron's attitude towards that religion was unusually sympathetic from the outset. In his poetry, in his letters, and in an address to Parliament, he supported Catholic emancipation. In this instance, however, we are more interested in his personal response, having taken up exile in Catholic Europe, and in particular Italy.

To begin with, it is notable that in contrast to his comments on his Calvinist past, his references to Catholicism are fairly expansive, largely positive, and even, on occasion, enthusiastic. A few examples will suffice to strike the tone. Speaking in 1821 of his daughter Allegra, he writes: 'It is besides my wish that she should be a Roman Catholic which I look upon as the best religion as it is assuredly the oldest of the various branches of Christianity.'[5] Again, he writes to Thomas Moore in 1882: 'I am no enemy of religion. As proof I'm educating my natural daughter a strict Catholic in a convent in Romagna: for I think people can never have *enough* of religion, if they are to have any. I incline, myself, very much to the Catholic doctrines.'[7] How genuine such statements are we can never be sure. A final example is perhaps particularly telling. Again writing to Moore, later in the same year, he states:

As I said before, I am really a great admirer of tangible religion; and am breeding one of my daughters a Catholic, that she may have her hands full. It is by far the most elegant worship, hardly excepting the Greek mythology. What with incense, pictures, statues, altars, shrines, relics, and the real presence, confession, absolution – there is something sensible to grasp at.[7]

This, together with the attributed statement, 'I have often wished I had been born a Catholic. That Purgatory of theirs is a comfortable doctrine',[8] would seem to suggest the essence of Byron's attraction to Catholicism, in the light of the psychological implications of Calvinist dogma. He is drawn precisely to those reconciliatory functions that his own religious background had denied him.

I think that there is a real attraction here to some degree, despite the occasional flippancy which it would be dishonest not to acknowledge. Thus, in the letter to Moore he continues: 'Besides, it leaves no possibility of doubt; for those who swallow their Deity, really and truly, in transubstantiation, can hardly find anything else otherwise than easy of digestion.' However, he goes on:

> I am afraid that this sounds flippant, but I do not mean it to be so; only my turn of mind is so given to taking things in the absurd point of view, that it breaks out in spite of me every now and then.

I think this letter strikes the balance. A degree of flippancy, of scepticism, is surely to be expected. A statement of blind faith would be infinitely more surprising. Quite apart from those aspects of his character already discussed, Byron inhabits a world that is post-Hume, post-Voltaire, and any discussion of belief must take place in the presence of alternatives. In such a world, the most sophisticated contemplation of the religious view is open to the charge of naïvety, even where it is the non-believer's understanding of belief that is the more naïve. The flippancy is perhaps simply an acknowledgement of this, and does not seem to contradict a degree of genuine attraction. Conversely, this is equally compatible with the conclusion that, all told, Byron probably remains a sceptic, when he is not a cynic to the last.

This is about as far as we can get in the matter of Byron's attitude to the Catholic religion. Insofar as religion appealed, Catholicism appealed, for reasons that may relate to his own Calvinist background. Just as we looked beyond Calvinism to the ambience it created, however, so beyond Catholicism we must consider the effect of the ambience created by Catholic Europe, and by Italy in particular. This, I should stress, is a matter distinct from religion, as we are speaking for the most part of influences of which no clergymen of whatever denomination would approve. As we are told in *Don Juan*:

'Tis a sad thing, I cannot choose but say,
    And all the fault of that indecent sun,
Who cannot leave alone our helpless clay,
    But will keep baking, broiling, burning on,
That howsoever people fast and pray
    The flesh is frail, and so the soul undone:
What men call gallantry, and gods adultery,
Is much more common where the climate's sultry.

Happy the nations of the moral North!
    Where all is virtue, and the winter season
Sends sin, without a rag on, shivering forth . . .[9]

The reasons for this contrast have to do with more than the weather. For Byron, northern morality is something held together by hypocrisy and cant, and it is their relative absence that he responds to in his Italian years.

It is interesting to speculate how far this in turn contributed to the full emergence of another poetic voice. It is worth considering how far the changing tone of the poetry itself, from the damned hero of *Childe Harold* to the urbane and cynical comedy of *Don Juan*, reflects the two contrasting psychological ambiences, and how far the emergence of the latter voice, reflects Italy's facilitation of Byron, a relatively accommodated man in what we might call a condition of secular Catholicism.

I have said at the outset that I have no particular axe to grind in this matter, and that I am conscious that the evidence is such as to remain fairly open ended. Nevertheless, it is an interesting area for speculation, not only in itself, but in relation to other aspects of Byron's background, as I hope this paper has suggested.

NOTES

1. Epigraph to *The Rime of the Ancient Mariner*, from *Archaeologiae Philosophicae*, Thomas Burnet, 1692.
2. Angus Calder, *Byron* (1984), 52.

3. Letter to William Gifford, 18 June 1813. *Byron's Letters and Journals*, ed. Leslie A. Marchand (1973–82), vol. 3, 64.

4. Letter to Annabella Milbanke, 26 September 1813, *BLJ*, vol. 3, 11.

5. Letter to Richard Belgrave Hoppner, 3 April 1821. *BLJ*, vol. 8, 98.

6. Letter to Thomas Moore, 4 March 1822. *BLJ*, vol. 9, 119.

7. Letter to Thomas Moore, 8 March 1822. *BLJ*, vol. 9, 123.

8. *Medwin's Conversations with Lord Byron*, Ernest J. Lovell Jnr (ed.), 1966.

9. *Don Juan*, Canto I, stanza 63.

Byron and Scott

P. H. SCOTT

At first glance, you might suppose that it would be hard to find two men more different and incompatible in character than Sir Walter Scott and Lord Byron. Scott, outwardly at least, was a prudent, douce, respectable Edinburgh lawyer, devoted to the Roman, and Scottish, virtues of effort, stoical endurance and self-control. *Agere atque pati Romanum est*, as he remarked in his *Journal*.[1] What would such a man have in common with the reckless, outrageous, passionate, indulgent, convention-defying Byron? Of course, the truth is the opposite from what one might expect. Each liked and admired the other to a degree which must be rare between two writers who were clear rivals for public favour.

Each expressed his feelings about the other as a man and a writer frequently and consistently. Scott of Byron, in a letter of 10 January 1817 to John Murray: 'No one can honour Lord Byron's poems more than I do and no one has so great a wish to love him personally'.[2] Byron of Scott in his *Journal* on 17 November 1813: 'I like the man – and admire his works to what Mr Braham calls *Entusymusy*'[3] In his *Journal* a few days later, he said that Scott was 'undoubtedly the Monarch of Parnassus' and placed him on the top of his 'Gradus ad Parnassum'.[4] Again in 1821:

> Scott is certainly the most wonderful writer of the day. His novels are a new literature in themselves, and his poetry is as good as any – if not better . . . I like him, too, for his manliness of character, for the extreme pleasantness of his conversation, and his good nature towards myself, person-ally. May he prosper for he deserves it. I know no reading to which I fall with such alacrity as a work of W. Scott's.[5]

Equally, Scott gives pride of place to Byron. He spoke of Byron's 'boundless Genius',[6] and said that he gave up writing

51

poetry because Byron beat him.[7] 'It is well for us', he remarked
in a letter to his publisher Cadell, 'that he has not turned
himself to tale telling, for he would have endangered our
supremacy in that department.'[8]

This relationship, 'warm and cordial on both sides', as Leslie
Marchand describes it,[9] began rather inauspiciously. Byron
published his *English Bards and Scotch Reviewers* in March 1809
anonymously, but it was no secret that he had written it. The
poem makes some mocking references to Scott's *Lay of the Last
Minstrel* and *Marmion* and accuses him of writing for money:

> And thinkst thou, Scott! by vain conceit perchance,
> On public taste to foist thy stale romance,
> Though Murray with his Miller may combine
> To yield thy muse just half-a-crown per line?
> No when the sons of song descend to trade,
> Their bays are sear, their former laurels fade.

Scott seems to have come across the poem in August when he
mentions it in the course of a letter to Robert Southey:

> In the meantime, it is funny enough to see a whelp of a
> young Lord Byron abusing me, of whose circumstances he
> knows nothing, for endeavouring to scratch out a living
> with my pen. God help the bear, if, having little else to eat,
> he must not even suck his own paws. I can assure the noble
> imp of fame it is not my fault that I was not born to a park and
> £5.000 a-year, as it is not his lordship's merit, although it
> may be his great good fortune, that he was not born to live
> by his literary talents or success.[10]

Scott evidently did not nurse a grievance, as many people
attacked like this would have done. Little more than a month
after the publication of Cantos I and II of Byron's *Childe
Harold's Pilgrimage* in February 1812, he was praising the poem
in letters to Joanna Baillie and J. B. S. Morritt. 'It is, I think, a
very clever poem', he wrote to the former, 'but gives no good
symptom of the writers heart or morals . . . I wish you would
read it.'[11] To Morritt his praise was even stronger, although he
still had reservations about the morality of the piece: 'Though
there is something provoking and insulting both to morality
and to feeling in his misanthropical ennui it gives nevertheless

an odd poignancy to his descriptions and reflections and upon the whole it is a poem of most extraordinary power and may rank its author with our first poets.'[12]

So far Scott and Byron had not met or even exchanged letters. They knew each other only by reputation and from their published works. As it happens, they were brought together very shortly after Scott had been writing these letters to his friends. Byron took the initiative, perhaps regretting his attack in *English Bards and Scotch Reviewers* or because of a generous impulse to tell Scott something which he know would please him. In June 1812, Byron had met the Prince Regent at an evening party where the Prince had talked about poetry at some length. He had displayed 'an intimacy and critical taste which at once surprised and delighted Lord Byron.' In particular, he spoke about Scott, whom he preferred 'far beyond every other poet of his time.' These phrases come from a letter from the publisher, John Murray, whom Byron had asked to pass on the report to Scott.[13] Scott responded by asking Murray to convey his thanks for this 'very handsome and gratifying communication', and took the opportunity to clear his name 'from any tinge of mercenary or sordid feeling in the eyes of a contemporary of genius.' He had *not* written *Marmion* under contract for a sum of money.[14] Thus encouraged, Byron replied by apologising for the satire, 'written when I was very young & very angry, & fully bent on displaying my wrath and my wit.'[15] In his reply, Scott invited Byron to visit Abbotsford, then a new and far from complete house.[16] From its beginning, their correspondence was friendly, warm and relaxed. Byron sent Scott a copy of his poem, *The Giaour* enscribed 'To the Monarch of Parnassus from one of his subjects'.[17]

In the event, Byron never visited Abbotsford, although Lady Byron did so in 1817. Eight years and much turmoil after the first invitation, Byron wrote from Ravenna to John Murray on 23 April 1820: 'My love to Scott . . . I hope to see him at Abbotsford before very long, and I will sweat his Claret for him'.[18] It was not to be. Their only meetings were in London in 1815 when Scott was passing through to and from Paris. Scott described them in a letter which he wrote in response to a

request from Tom Moore for facts and recollections which
would help him with his *Life* of Byron. It is worth quoting at
length because it says so much about Scott and Byron:
It was in the spring of 1815, that, chancing to be in
London, I had the advantage of a personal introduction to
Lord Byron. Report had prepared me to meet a man of
peculiar habits and a quick temper, and I had some doubts
whether we were likely to suit each other in society. I was
most agreeably disappointed in this respect. I found Lord
Byron in the highest degree courteous, and even kind. We
met for an hour or two almost daily, in Mr. Murray's
drawing-room, and found a great deal to say to each other.
We also met frequently in parties and evening society, so
that for about two months I had the advantage of a
considerable intimacy with this distinguished individual.
Our sentiments agreed a good deal, except upon the
subjects of religion and politics, upon neither of which I was
inclined to believe that Lord Byron entertained very fixed
opinions . . .
On politics, he used sometimes to express a high strain of
what is now called Liberalism; but it appeared to me that the
pleasure it afforded him, as a vehicle for displaying his wit
and satire against individuals in office, was at the bottom of
this habit of thinking, rather than any real conviction of the
political principles on which he talked. He was certainly
proud of his rank and ancient family, and, in that respect, as
much an aristocrat as was consistent with good sense and
good breeding. Some disgusts, how adopted I know not,
seemed to me to have given this peculiar and (as it appeared
to me) contradictory cast of mind; but at heart, I would have
termed Byron a patrician on principle.
Lord Byron's reading did not seem to have been very
extensive, either in poetry or history. Having the advantage
of him in that respect, and possessing a good competent
share of such reading as is little read, I was sometimes able to
put under his eye objects which had for him the interest of
novelty. I remember particularly repeating to him the fine
poem of Hardyknute, an imitation of the old Scottish ballad,
with which he was so much affected, that some one who

was in the same apartment asked me what I could possibly have been telling Byron by which he was so much agitated.

I saw Byron for the last time in 1815, after I returned from France. He dined, or lunched, with me at Long's, in Bond Street. I never saw him so full of gayety and good-humor . . .

Several letters passed between us – one perhaps every half-year. Like the old heroes in Homer, we exchanged gifts. I gave Byron a beautiful dagger mounted with gold, which had been the property of the redoubted Elfi Bey. But I was to play the part of Diomed in the Iliad, for Byron sent me, some time after, a large sepulchral vase of silver. It was full of dead men's bones . . .

I think I also remarked in Byron's temper starts of suspicion, when he seemed to pause and consider whether there had not been a secret, and perhaps offensive, meaning in something casually said to him. In this case, I also judged it best to let his mind, like a troubled spring, work itself clear, which it did in a minute or two. I was considerably older, you will recollect, than my noble friend, and had no reason to fear his misconstruing my sentiments towards him, nor had I ever the slightest reason to doubt that they were kindly returned on his part. If I had occasion to be mortified by the display of genius which threw into the shade such pretensions as I was then supposed to possess, I might console myself that, in my own case, the materials of mental happiness had been mingled in a greater proportion.[19]

Scott retained warm memories of his last meeting with Byron, which was on 14 September 1815.[20] Ten years later he referred to it in his *Journal*: 'I never saw Byron so full of fun, frolic, wit and whim: he was as playful as a kitten'.[21] But playful or not, Byron was then in the middle of his disastrous marriage. During the scandal of the separation which followed, almost all of Scott's correspondents took the side of Lady Byron.[22] Joanna Baillie even tried to persuade him to intervene over the financial settlement, since there was nobody, she said, whose good opinion Byron was more anxious to preserve.[23] Scott regretted the breakdown of the marriage, but he refused to be stampeded into the general mood of condemnation. 'I was in great hopes', he told Morritt in February 1816, 'that the comfort of domestic security might tame the wayward irregularity of mind which is unfortunately for its owner connected with such splendid talent. I have known Lord Byron to do very great and generous things and I would have been most happy to find that he had adopted other and more settled habits'.[24] In another letter to Morritt in May: 'Lord Byron with high genius and many points of a noble and generous feeling has Child Harolded himself and Outlawd himself into too great a resemblance with the picture of his imagination'.[25]

Byron left Britain in April 1816 to escape both the bailiffs and the weight of public disapproval. By the end of June he had written the third canto of *Childe Harold* and it was published by John Murray in November. Scott responded by writing a review of some thirty pages for the *Quarterly* (published in February 1817). He knew that he was taking a risk. The poem was so autobiographical in content that it was impossible to comment on it without saying something about Byron's personal situation, and, as he told Murray, he did not want to cause him pain.[26] The review praised Byron for his 'wide, powerful and original view of poetry' and suggested that his 'family misfortunes' were the consequences of 'a powerful and unbridled imagination, . . .the author and architect of its own disappointments'. Scott concluded with the 'anxious wish and eager hope' that Byron would recover peace of mind for the exercise of his 'splendid talents'.[27] At any time this would have been a kind and understanding review. In the circumstances, the writing of it was not only delicate and tactful, but courageous.

Byron was deeply touched. 'He must be a gallant as well as a good man,' he wrote to Murray in March 'who has ventured in that place – and at this time – to write such an article anonymously . . . It is not the mere praise, but there is a *tact* & a *delicacy* throughout not only with regard to me – but to *others*'.[28] A week later he had heard that Scott was the author and wrote to Thomas Moore, 'you will agree with me that such an article is still more honourable to him than to myself'.[29] Byron never forgot this example of Scott's courage and generosity. He mentioned it in a letter to Scott for the first time in January 1822: 'You went out of your way in 1817 – to do me a service when it required not merely kindness – but courage to do so . . . The very *tardiness* of this acknowledgement will at least show that I have not forgotten the obligation'.[30] On 29 May 1823, when Byron was preparing to leave Italy for his final journey to Greece, he took time to write to Henri Beyle (Stendhal). Beyle had praised Scott's writing in a pamphlet but said that 'his character is little worthy of enthusiasm'. Byron rose to his defence:

I have known Walter Scott long and well, and in occasional situations which call forth the *real* character – and I can assure you that his character *is* worthy of admiration – that of all men he is the most *open*, the most *honourable*, the most *amiable*. With his politics I have nothing to do: they differ from mine, which renders it difficult for me to speak of them. But he is *perfectly sincere* in them . . . *Believe* the *truth*. I say that Walter Scott is as nearly a thorough good man as man can be, because I *know* it by experience to be the case.[31]

There cannot be much doubt that when he wrote these words the *Quarterly* article was in his mind.

Scott proved his robust support for Byron once again by accepting in December 1821 the dedication of one of his boldest works, *Cain*. In his letter of acceptance to Murray, Scott said that 'Byron matched Milton on his own ground. Some part of the language is bold, and may shock one class of readers . . . But then they must condemn the Paradise Lost, if they have a mind to be consistent.'[32]

Byron's admiration for Scott as a writer was based at first on his poetry, but he became a great enthusiast for the novels as soon as he discovered them. The first of them, *Waverley*, was published on 7 July 1814. As early as the 24th of the same month Byron wrote to Murray: 'Waverley is the best and most interesting novel I have read since – I don't know when . . . besides – it is all easy to me – because I have been in Scotland so much – (though then young enough too) and feel at home with the people lowland & Gael.'[33] From then onwards Byron read all of Scott's novels as they appeared and, by his own repeated account, many times over. He said that he liked no reading so well.[34] Although they were still anonymous, 'by the author of Waverley', Byron seems never to have had any doubts that Scott was the 'great unknown'. In a letter of February 1820, for instance: 'I have more of Scott's novels (for surely they are Scott's) since we met, and am more and more delighted. I think I even prefer them to his poetry.'[35] Or in his *Journal* on 5 January 1821: 'Read the conclusion, for the fiftieth time (I have read all W. Scott's novels at least fifty times) of the third series of "Tales of my Landlord", – grand work – Scotch Fielding, as well as great English poet – wonderful man I long to get drunk with him.'[36]

From 1814 to the end of his life Byron's letters are full of allusions to the novels, praise of them, and requests to Murray to be sure to send new ones as they were published. There are also frequent quotations from them, usually phrases of the dialogue in Scots, which show how familiar he was with them and how much at home with Scots vocabulary. He wrote to Scott himself about them from Pisa on 12 January 1822:

I don't like to bore you about the Scotch novels (as they call them though two of them are wholly English – and the rest half so) but nothing can or could ever persuade me since I was the first ten minutes in your company that you are *not* the Man . . . To me those novels have so much of "Auld lang syne". (I was bred a canny Scot till ten years old) that I never move without them – and when I removed from Ravenna to Pisa the other day – and sent on my library before – they were the only books that I kept by me – although I already knew them by heart . . . I need not add that I would be delighted to see you again – which is far more than I shall ever feel or say for England or (with a few exceptions of "kith – kin – and allies") any thing that it contains . . . But my "heart warms to the Tartan" or to any thing of Scotland.[37]

Byron's response to the Waverley novels helps to explain the evident affinity between him and Scott. In his *Journal*, Scott describes himself as 'tolerably national'.[38] This was a calculated understatement, because Scott's passion for Scotland was a dominant force in his composition.[39] I think that there is strong evidence that Byron too was 'tolerably national', if not to the same overwhelming degree as Scott. In his essay on Byron, T. S. Eliot said that Byron was a Scottish poet, and in comparing him with Scott remarked: 'Possibly Byron, who must have thought of himself as an English poet, was the more Scotch of the two because of being unconscious of his true nationality.'[40] On the contrary, I think that Byron makes it very clear, as in the letters just quoted, that he was perfectly conscious of his Scottishness.

Indeed when Byron said in Canto X of *Don Juan* that he was 'half a Scot by birth, and bred a whole one',[41] he was speaking the literal truth. He was 'half a Scot' because his mother was Scottish; he was 'bred a whole one' because he spent the first ten years of his life in Aberdeen and was educated at the Grammar School. I think it is generally agreed that the first few years of life are the most influential in determining character and attitudes. Many people, including Eliot and Grierson, have noted the influence on him of Scottish Calvinism.[42] It is also quite certain that he heard all around him in Aberdeen, and learned to speak, good Buchan Scots. His frequent quotation in his letters of phrases in Scots shows how he responded to it. No doubt he acquired an English veneer at Harrow and Cambridge; but, as Eliot says, he 'remained oddly alien' in English society.[43] I think that is because he was fundamentally Scottish.

There is a significant episode in Byron's correspondence with his half-sister, Augusta Leigh. She wrote in February 1817 to congratulate him on the assumption that he was 'P.P.' By this she meant Peter Pattieson, the fictitious character to whom Scott attributed *Tales of My Landlord*, the four volumes published in December, 1816, which contained *The Black Dwarf* and *Old Mortality*. The books had not yet reached Byron in Venice and he had no idea what Augusta was talking about. 'I am not P.P.', he replied, 'and I assure you upon my honour – & do not understand to what book you allude – so that all your compliments are quite thrown away.'[44] However after he had read the *Tales*, he wrote to John Murray in May: 'The *Tales of My Landlord* I have read with great pleasure – & perfectly understand why my sister & aunt are so very positive in the very erroneous persuasion that they must have been written by me – if you knew me as well as they do – you would perhaps have fallen into the same mistake.'[45]

In his footnote to the first of these two letters, Leslie Marchand suggests that Augusta was misled by the character of David Ritchie in *The Black Dwarf* who was 'haunted by a consciousness of his own deformity'. Certainly, it is quite possible that this resemblance to Byron triggered off her conclusion. (Incidentally, another bond between Scott and Byron was, of course, that they were both lame and both compensated for their handicap by vigorous physical activity, Byron by his swimming and Scott on horseback.) But this point alone could hardly have led anyone to imagine that Byron was the author, unless they could also suppose he was capable of writing anything so essentially Scottish as these two novels and of writing superb dialogue in Scots. Although the *Tales* were not attributed on the title page to the 'author of Waverley', it was very clear to everyone that they were by the same writer. The implication of Augusta's conclusion, and of Byron's understanding of it, was that he was Scottish enough to be conceivable as the author of the first six, and some of the most Scottish, of the Waverley novels.

Yet another quality which Byron and Scott shared, and which they recognised and appreciated in each other, was a general approach to life which might seem inconsistent with their reputation as leaders of European romanticism. In a letter to Murray in March 1817, Byron said of Scott: 'He & Gifford & Moore are the only *regulars* I ever knew who had nothing of the *Garrison* about their manner – no nonsense – nor affectations look you.'[46] Elsewhere, he refers to Scott as a man of the world.[47] Scott said very much the same of Byron: 'What I liked about Byron, besides his boundless genius, was his generosity of spirit as well as purse, and his utter contempt of all affectations of literature.'[48] Scott was delighted by a story which Moore told him about Byron: 'While they stood at the window of Byron's Palazzo in Venice looking at a beautiful sunset, Moore was naturally led to say something of its beauty, when Byron answered in a tone that I can easily conceive, 'Ah come, d-n me, Tom, don't be poetical'.[49]

This feet-on-the-ground, no-nonsense attitude is remote from the Byronic hero, but it is entirely consistent with the

realistic, and sceptical attitude, the eighteenth-century rationalism, which formed one aspect of both Byron and Scott. Both
had been educated in cities, Aberdeen and Edinburgh, where
the atmosphere of the Scottish Enlightenment prevailed and it
left its influence on both of them. Its co-existence with
romanticism of diverse kinds might perhaps be an example of
what Gregory Smith called 'the Caledonian antisyzygy' and
identified as the 'combination of opposites', or 'the contrasts
which the Scot shows at every turn.'[50]

Another obvious link between the two men is, of course,
that they both wrote long, narrative poems. There are many
similarities in metre, style and manner, even if the setting and
content is very different and if Byron eventually added a new
dimension to this kind of writing. Byron probably got the idea
of writing poems of this kind because of Scott's example.
Lockhart had no doubt that this was so: 'indeed in all his early
serious narratives, Byron owed at least half his success to
clever though perhaps unconscious imitation of Scott.'[51]
Lockhart has another anecdote which shows how closely the
minds of the two poets sometimes resembled one another. In
London in 1828, he was with Scott listening to Mrs Arkwright
singing some of her own settings. After one of them, Scott
whispered to him 'Capital words – whose are they? – Byron's I
suppose, but I don't remember them.' Lockhart continues, 'He
was astonished when I told him that they were his own in *The
Pirate*. He seemed pleased at the moment, but said next minute
– "You have distressed me – if memory goes, all is up with me,
for that was always my strong point".'[51]

Before Byron decided in 1823 to go to Greece to help in their
revolution, he had considered other possibilities. In 1819 he
had thought in particular of South America, where states were
struggling for their independence.[53] In May 1822 he asked
John Murray to send him the *Lockhart Papers*, 'a publication
upon Scotch affairs of some time since'.[54] The papers were the
Memoirs of John Lockhart of Carnwath, a member of the
Scottish Parliament from 1703 to 1707 and a strong opponent of
the Union with England. Byron did not say why he wanted the
books, but since they contain the best contemporary exposure
of the sordid transaction of the Union, it might be that he

thought also of Scotland as a country where an independence movement might be stimulated or encouraged.

But, of course, it was Greece that he chose, and there he died on 19 April 1823. When the news reached Edinburgh, Scott wrote an obituary for the *Edinburgh Weekly Journal*, calling Byron, 'That mighty genius, which walked among men as something superior to ordinary mortality, and whose powers we beheld with wonder and something approaching to terror.'[55] So ended a relationship which did credit to both men and gave much pleasure and satisfaction to both of them. During the rest of his life, Scott's thoughts often turned to Byron: 'I very often think of him almost with tears', he told Moore in August 1825.[56] Once, shortly after Byron's death, he imagined for a moment that he saw him 'with wonderful accuracy' standing in the hall at Abbotsford.[57] He summed up his view of Byron in his Journal: 'This was the man – quaint, capricious, and playful, with all his immense genius. He wrote from impulse never from effort and therefore I have always reckond Burns and Byron the most genuine poetical genuises of my time and half a century before me.'[58] In 1832, as Scott was himself close to death and was hurrying home to Abbotsford from Italy, he visited Venice and went to see the balcony on which Byron had said to Moore, 'Damn me, Tom, don't be poetical.'[59]

ABBREVIATIONS

J.   Sir Walter Scott, *Journal* (Edinburgh, 1950)
G.   *The Letters of Sir Walter Scott*, ed. H. J. C. Grierson, 12 vols
      (London, 1932–37)
M.   *Byron's Letters and Journals*, ed. Leslie A. Marchand,
      12 vols (London, 1973–82)
L.   J. G. Lockhart, *Memoirs of Sir Walter Scott*, 5 vols (London,
      1900)

NOTES

1.   J.   22 June 1826
2.   G.   IV, 365
3.   M.   III, 209
4.   M.   III, 219–20

5. M. VIII, 23
6. J. 23 November 1825
7. L. V, 391
8. Edgar Johnson, *Sir Walter Scott, The Great Unknown* (New York, 1970), II, 1219 (quoting a letter from Scott to Cadell)
9. M. IV, 358
10. G. II, 214
11. G. III, 98–9
12. G. III, 114–15
13. G. III, 135 f.n. 1
14. G. III, 135–9
15. M. II, 182
16. G. III, 140–1
17. L. II, 508
18. M. VII, 83
19. L. II, 514–17
20. L. III, 24
21. J. 21 December 1825
22. Wilfred Partington, *Sir Walter's Post-Bag* (London, 1932), 114
23. Ibid., 116
24. G. IV, 184
25. G. IV, 234
26. G. IV, 364–5
27. *Quarterly Review*, XVI, dated October 1816 (but published in February 1817), 189, 207, 208
28. M. V, 178
29. M. V, 185
30. M. IX, 85–6
31. M. X, 189–90
32. G. VII, 37
33. M. IV, 146
34. M. VII, 48
35. M. VII, 45
36. M. VIII, 13
37. M. IX, 86–7
38. J. 22 November 1825
39. See Chapter 7 of my *Walter Scott and Scotland* (Edinburgh, 1981)
40. T. S. Eliot, 'Byron' in *From Anne to Victoria; Essays by Various Hands* (1937), 602
41. Stanza XVII
42. T. S. Eliot, op. cit., 604; Herbert Grierson, *The Background of English Literature* (1962), 152.
43. T. S. Eliot, op. cit., 617.
44. M. V, 171
45. M. V, 220

46. M.   V, 192
47. M.   IX, 30
48. J.   23 November 1825
49. J.   9 February 1826
50. G. Gregory Smith, *Scottish Literature: Character and Influence*
     (1919), 4
51. L.   II, 509
52. L.   V, 195–6 f.n.
53. M.   VI, 123 f.n. 1; 212
54. M.   IX, 156.
55. Sir Walter Scott, *Miscellaneous Prose* (Edinburgh, 1834),
     II, 343
56. G.   IX, 199
57. L.   V, 131–2 and f.n. 57;   J.   9 February 1826
58. J.   9 February 1826
59. Edgar Johnson, op. cit., II, 1248.

The Provost and his Lord: John Galt and Lord Byron

MARGERY MCCULLOCH

John Galt first met Lord Byron in Gibraltar in 1809. Both were attempting to escape the frustrations of London. Galt was a Scot, born and brought up in his early years in the Ayrshire town of Irvine – the 'Gudetown' of his novel *The Provost*. His family later moved to Greenock to take advantage of the prosperity of that increasingly thriving port, and Galt's first employment was in the world of commerce. He was an unusual business man, however, in that from his beginnings literary activity went hand in hand with business activity. Like many ambitious Scots in the nineteenth century, he soon found his way to London, where at first he was conspicuously successful neither in business nor in literature. His travels in Europe between 1809 and 1811, which provided a significant part of the material for his biography of Lord Byron, were in part an attempt to recover his nervous health after the failure of his business ventures and literary aspirations.

Byron – 'half a Scot by birth'[1] through his mother's family – had also left England in a state of disaffection. He had recently taken his seat in the House of Lords unaccompanied by supporters and after some initial difficulty in establishing his credentials. His collection of poems *Hours of Idleness* had been devastatingly dismissed by the *Edinburgh Review* in what Galt called 'bleak and blighting criticism'.[2] Unlike Galt, however, he had at least the satisfaction of leaving England in some notoriety, his satirical reply to the *Review* – *English Bards and Scotch Reviewers* – having attracted much attention and a rapid sale.

The impulse behind this essay, then, is John Galt's *The Life of Lord Byron*, written and published in 1830 and based largely on his meeting and travels with Byron in the Eastern Mediterranean between 1809 and 1811; and the associations and reflections it has aroused in my own mind with regard to both author and subject, especially with regard to Byron's personality and poetry.

Galt's first sighting of Byron – whom he did not at that point recognise – was in the garrison library in Gibraltar:

> . . . a young man came in and seated himself opposite to me at the table where I was reading. Something in his appearance attracted my attention. His dress indicated a Londoner of some fashion, partly by its neatness and simplicity, with just so much of a peculiarity of style as served to show, that although he belonged to the order of metropolitan beaux, he was not altogether a common one.
>
> I thought his face not unknown to me; I began to conjecture where I could have seen him; and, after an unobserved scrutiny, to speculate both as to his character and vocation. His physiognomy was pre-possessing and intelligent, but ever and anon his brows lowered and gathered; a habit, as I then thought, with a degree of affectation in it, probably first assumed for picturesque effect and energetic expression; but which I afterwards discovered was undoubtedly the occasional scowl of some unpleasant reminiscence: it was certainly disagreeable – forbidding – but still the general cast of his features was impressed with elegance and character.   (59-60)

Later, having discovered the identity of the young man and having embarked with him and his travelling companion, Hobhouse, for Sardinia, Galt observes Byron's adoption of a demeanour which anticipates that of his hero, Childe Harold:

> Hobhouse, with more of the commoner, made himself one of the passengers at once; but Byron held himself aloof, and sat on the rail, leaning on the mizzen shrouds, inhaling, as it were poetical sympathy, from the gloomy rock, then dark and stern in the twilight.   (61)

In these early observations of Byron one can recognise the eye and mind of the creator of Micah Balwhidder and Provost Pawkie of Gudetown. Galt makes it clear at the outset of his biography that there will be no sensational preoccupation with or prying into Byron's personal life. Instead, he will confine himself 'as much as practicable, consistent with the end in view, to an outline of his Lordship's intellectual features' (iii), and will attempt to 'consider him . . . as his character will be estimated when contemporary surmises are forgotten, and when the monument he has raised to himself is contemplated for its beauty and magnificence, without suggesting recollections of the eccentricities of the builder' (4).

Galt is a discerning biographer and the course he adopts accords well with his own qualities as a writer and man. As with the relations between Provost Pawkie and *his* lord, Galt is courteous but never subservient towards Lord Byron. Indeed, there is more than a little of Pawkie's canniness in the following report of Byron's touchiness and Galt's humouring of him after a theatrical performance in Cagliari:

When the performance was over, Mr Hill came down with Lord Byron to the gate of the upper town, where his Lordship, as we were taking leave, thanked him with more elocution than was precisely requisite. The style and formality of the speech amused Mr Hobhouse, as well as others; and when the minister retired, he began to rally his Lordship on the subject. But Byron really fancied that he had acquitted himself with grace and dignity, and took the jocularity of his friend amiss – a little banter ensued – the poet became petulant, and Mr Hobhouse walked on; while Byron, on account of his lameness, and the roughness of the pavement, took hold of my arm, appealing to me, if he could have said less, after the kind and hospitable treatment we had all received. Of course, though I thought pretty much as Mr Hobhouse did, I could not do otherwise than civilly assent, especially as his Lordship's comfort, at the moment, seemed in some degree dependent on being confirmed in the good opinion he was desirous to entertain of his own courtesy. From that night I evidently rose in his good graces; and, as he was always most agreeable and interesting when familiar, it was worth my while to advance, but by cautious circumvallations, into his intimacy; for his uncertain temper made his favour precarious.   (66)

It should be said that Byron's sentiments, at that time, did not exactly accord with Galt's. He is reported by Lady Blessington as regretting that he had not truly appreciated Galt during these early meetings: 'his manner had not deference enough for my then aristocratical taste, and finding I could not awe him into respect sufficiently profound for my sublimer self either as a peer or an author, I felt a little grudge towards him . . .'[3]

Galt, on the other hand, is objective and fair in his portrait of Byron. He provides the reader with the kind of precise, relevant detail of events which enables one to enter into the happenings and form one's own judgements. He is also, as one would expect from his fiction, psychologically perceptive and looks below the surface petulance of his subject to the insecurity and sensitivity within. Byron's behaviour might often display 'the pride of rank' (154), but Galt's portrait shows us a man whose insecurity made him 'so skinless in sensibility as respected himself, and so distrustful in his universal apprehensions of human nature, as respected others' (175).

There seems to have been an intuitive understanding of Byron on Galt's part, an unforced sympathetic feeling for the man. It is interesting to note that while he always seeks out a psychological explanation for Byron's capriciousness, Galt has little patience with the unconventional ideas and behaviour of Shelley, with whom Byron later became friendly. While lamenting that Byron had 'a wayward delight in magnifying his excesses, not in what was to his credit, like most men, but in what was calculated to do him no honour' (224), Galt dismisses Shelley as having 'a singular incapability of conceiving the existing state of things as it practically affects the nature and conditions of man' (255). Nor could Shelley's work provide, for Galt, a counter-balance to his behaviour, as did Byron's. For Galt, Shelley's 'works were sullied with the erroneous induction of an understanding which, in as much as he regarded all the existing world in the wrong, must be considered as having been either shattered or defective' (256-7). Shelley, in Galt's view, 'was more of a metaphysician than a poet' (257).

Despite the differences in the character and life-style of Galt and Byron, there are significant underlying similarities which would have worked towards Galt's understanding of his subject. Both were role-players in their work, Galt through the adoption of such personae as Balwhidder and Pawkie, Byron through his diverse poetic voices. Both were enemies of hypocrisy and were to become masters of the ironic presentation of self-delusion. There is, however, less of what Galt called Byron's 'gratuitous spleen' (190) in his own work, while Byron is reported by Lady Blessington to have said of Galt's novels that what he admired particularly 'is that with a perfect knowledge of human nature and its frailties and legerdemain tricks, he shows a tenderness of heart which convinces me that *his* is in the right place, and he has a sly caustic humour that is very amusing.'[4] This is a fair comment on Galt's presentation of a character such as Provost Pawkie, for however devious and self-reflexive that politician's activities may be, they are also on the whole directed towards the improvement of the community and are conducted with a sound common sense which points to his author's Enlightenment affinities.

This affinity with the eighteenth century is another bond between the two writers. Byron's alienated, angst-ful protagonists have become the archetypes of what we call 'the Romantic hero', but Byron himself looked to another age for *his* poetic heroes. The narrator's credo in Canto I of *Don Juan* is 'Thou shalt believe in Milton, Dryden, Pope;/Thou shalt not set up Wordsworth, Coleridge, Southey' (stanza 205); and although the attacks on the Lakers in *Don Juan* have the verve and pointedness of a current preoccupation, Byron's published disdain for their work and his admiration for the earlier Milton, Dryden and Pope, goes back as far as the 1809 *English Bards and Scotch Reviewers.*

Galt criticised Byron for aiming his satire too generally in that early work, but he himself shows a similar antipathy to the kind of sensibility epitomised by the 'gelatinous' Lakers, as he calls them in the biography (41). Most readers of Byron are familiar with the passage in Canto I of *Don Juan* where Juan for the first time feels the stirrings of love – what Galt was wont to call 'the passion' – but because his mother has edited out natural history from his education, he is unable to understand what is wrong with him. In his account of Juan's sufferings, Byron wittily combines an attack on the hypocrisy of educational attitudes with allusions to Wordsworth's philosophy of

nature, and with an ironic backward glance at his own Byronic
heroes. In his characteristic fashion he builds up the portrait of
his man of unfocused feeling stanza by stanza, accumulating
detail and just when it seems about to reach its sublime climax,
he undercuts the effect with a bathetic final line:

> He pored upon the leaves, and on the flowers,
>   And heard a voice in all the winds; and then
> He thought of wood nymphs and immortal bowers,
>   And how the goddesses came down to men:
> He miss'd the pathway, he forgot the hours,
>   And when he look'd upon his watch again,
> He found how much old Time had been a winner –
> He also found that he had lost his dinner.   (stanza 94)

Significant in the context of the relationship between Galt
and Byron is a similarly comic passage from Galt's *Annals of the
Parish*, where the Revd Balwhidder attempts to mitigate his
grief at the loss of his first wife. Initially he occupies his mind
by the erecting of a monument and the composing of an
epitaph, but being once again in danger of 'sinking into the
hyperchonderies', Balwhidder follows Wordsworth and Juan
and 'often walked in the fields, and held communion with
nature and wondered at the mysteries thereof.'[5] This inspired
communing in turn leads him to think of writing a book, but
finally common sense and Providence intervene to persuade
him to take another wife, as Galt – like Byron – deflects his
romantic musings with a domestic crisis which demands a
more down-to-earth, social resolution. In the absence of a
mistress, Balwhidder's 'servant lasses . . . wastered everything
at such a rate, and made such a galravitching in the house,
that, long before the end of the year, the year's stipend was all
spent.' Worse still, 'one of my lassies had got herself with
bairn, which was an awful thing to think had happened in the
house of her master, and that master a minister of the Gospel.'[6]
In the face of these worldly disasters, Balwhidder gives up
'sauntering along the edge of Eglesham Wood, looking at the
industrious bee going from flower to flower, and the idle
butterfly, that layeth up no store, but perisheth ere it is
winter',[7] and sets about the search for a prudent helpmate.

Thus reason and good sense, a little tinged with self-delusion, triumph as in Byron over contemplation and the mysteries of the natural world.

This preference for Enlightenment good sense as opposed to the sensibility associated with Wordsworth and the Lakers is in evidence throughout Galt's biography of Byron. Speaking of the poet's early childhood in Aberdeenshire, Galt rejects theories which ascribe his poetic genius to his early association with the natural world. Yet, paradoxically, his accompanying comment that 'deep feelings of dissatisfaction and disappoint- ment are . . . the very spirit of his works, and a spirit of such qualities is the least of all likely to have arisen from the contemplation of magnificent nature, or to have been inspired by studying her storms or serenity' (19) takes us into the world of Wordsworth's 'Michael' or 'Resolution and Independence', where nature provides consolation and strength for the disquieted spirit. To the twentieth-century reader, Galt's viewpoint that Byron's delight 'in contemplating the Malvern Hills, was not because they resembled the scenery of Lochyna- gar, but because they awoke trains of thought and fancy, associated with recollections of that scenery,' brings him close to a perception of Wordsworth's poetic method, as does his further comment that the 'poesy of the feeling lay not in the beauty of the objects, but in the moral effect of the traditions, to which these objects served as talisman of the memory' (28).

In effect, Galt, like Byron, has affinities with both the Enlightenment and the Romantic periods in his attitude to the nature of poetry. Perhaps because of the different cultural and social ambience from which he came, and the nature of a literary tradition which in the eighteenth century produced Fergusson and Burns as opposed to Pope, Galt, unlike the aristocratically-inclined and Harrow-educated Byron, could more readily accommodate Wordsworth's insistence that 'a poet is a man speaking to men' and using the language 'really used by men.'[8] With Galt, however, there is an emphasis on the 'worldly' and the social not to be found in Wordsworth, which relates to the eighteenth-century conception of the poet's social role. In Galt's view, 'the greatest poets have all been men – worldly men, different only from others in

reasoning, more by feeling than induction.' He stresses that
no greater misconception has ever been obtruded upon the
world as philosophic criticism, than the theory of poets
being the offspring of 'cooing lambs and capering doves'
. . . The most vigorous poets, those who have influenced
longest and are most quoted, have indeed been all men of
great shrewdness of remark, and any thing but your
chin-on-hand contemplators . . . Are there any symptoms of
the gelatinous character of the effusions of the Lakers in the
compositions of Homer?

He has no doubt as to where the poet should find the material
for his work:

Compare, the poets that babble of green fields with those
who deal in the actions of men, such as Shakespeare, and it
must be confessed that it is not those who have looked at
external nature who are the true poets, but those who have
seen and considered most about the business and bosom of
man. It may be an advantage that a poet should have the
benefit of landscapes and storms, as children are the better
for country air and cow's milk; but the true scene of their
manly work and business is in the populous city.   (40-2)

Such a comment is reminiscent of Byron's attacks on
Wordsworth, Coleridge and Southey. Although Byron condemned them as 'epic renegades', ostensibly for turning Tory
(*Don Juan*, Dedication, I), one senses that, like Galt, he had an
innate dislike of the formal and philosophical nature of the
attempt to 'make it new' by these older Romantics. Again like
Galt, Byron is inevitably a man of his time, and, despite his
dislike of Wordsworth's poetic method, in *Don Juan* and *The
Vision of Judgment* especially he employs the everyday language and everyday subjects (although from a higher social
stratum) which Wordsworth advocated. Yet, as with his
biographer, he is strongly affiliated to the eighteenth-century
concept of the social role of the artist and the artist as
craftsman. Pope's 'Know then thyself, presume not God to
scan,/The proper study of mankind is man'[9] has much
relevance to the work and attitudes of both Galt and Byron.
Childe Harold may seem to be at one with Wordsworth's
solitary protagonists, shunning society and communing with

the natural world, nevertheless society is an ever-present touchstone in Byron's poetry as it is not in Wordsworth's. The society Harold rejects is always with us, as a result of his constantly expressed alienation from it. Similarly, the natural world serves not as a substitute for society, but as a reminder of Harold's parting from that society. In his observations on Byron in Athens and Ephesus, Galt comments that 'Lord Byron made almost daily excursions on horseback chiefly for exercise and to see the localities of celebrated spots. He affected to have no taste for the arts, and he certainly took but little pleasure in the examination of the ruins' (120). In Galt's view, Byron's imagination was one which 'required the action of living characters to awaken its dormant sympathies' (137).

Yet, although he looked to Pope for many of his poetic values, Byron's social satires reveal the dissimilarity in their worlds. However critical Pope may be of his society's morality and attitudes in action, his criticism comes from a stable base within that society. At root he and his society have the same moral values, and he can expect to find an audience. The situation is otherwise with Byron. Superficially his verse satires may remind one of Pope, but his is the comedy of manners of a subversive outsider, who knows that his views will outrage even while they entertain. Nor is there any sense in Byron's poetry of a reforming purpose, of a shock administered in order to return the audience to the ideal of shared values. Like his alienated, wandering heroes, Byron himself, even at his most entertaining and uncensorious, seems set apart from the society he observes and caricatures. This sense of apartness is something we do not find in Galt. Despite the long periods he spent outside Scotland – in London, Europe and later in Canada – and despite the problems of Scottish national and cultural identity brought about by the two Unions with England, Galt's ironic, dramatic enactments of Scottish small town and parish life are the work of an insider, who appears to be proceeding from a stable base within his society.

In addition to his observations on Byron the man, Galt makes acute comments throughout his biography on the nature of Byron's poetry. One of these is his recurring insistence that Byron's best poetry is based on factual experience and not on imagination. For Galt, unlike Coleridge, memory is not allied with fancy as a lower form of creative activity, but is the very corner-stone of such activity. Galt parted from Byron and Hobhouse at Malta in the autumn of 1809, and did not meet up with them again until the following spring in Athens. He continues his account of Byron's travels during this period by references to the detail of *Childe Harold's Pilgrimage*, supported by his reading of Byron's and Hobhouse's accounts of their journeyings and his own memories of their conversations. By using *Childe Harold* in this way, he gives substance to his contention that Byron's is a poetry based on fact and experience which demonstrates 'how little, after all, of great invention is requisite to make interesting and magnificent poetry' (102).

It would be wrong, however, to see Galt as the kind of commentator who insists on a direct correspondence between Byron's poetry and his life: he is well aware that the use to which experience is put is part of the transforming imaginative process. Byron's own journey from the town of Joannina to Zitza in search of the vizier Ali Pashaw is seen to parallel that of his hero Childe Harold, as does his kind reception by the prior of the monastery where the travellers seek shelter for the night. On the other hand, Galt comments that while 'many traits and lineaments of Lord Byron's own character may be traced in the portraits of his heroes, I have yet often thought that Ali Pashaw was the model from which he drew several of their most remarkable features' (88). In a piece of Pawkie-like self-advertisement, Galt describes Byron's encounter with Ali Pashaw – 'the Rob Roy of Albania' (89) – not only through the detail of *Childe Harold* but also through his memories of his own reception by Ali Pashaw's son at Tripolizza, justifying the inclusion of his experience with the comment that 'the ceremonies on such visits are similar all over Turkey, among personages of the same rank' (84).

One passage from Byron's poetry which exudes the exotic flamboyance of Hollywood invention, but which Galt maintains has its origins in a witnessed event, is the description of the dogs devouring the dead in *The Siege of Corinth*:

From a Tartar's skull they had stripped the flesh,
As ye peel the fig when its fruit is fresh;
And their white tusks crunched o'er the whiter skull,
As it slipped through the jaws, when their edge grew dull,
As they lazily mumbled the bones of the dead,
When they scarce could rise from the spot where they fed;
So well had they broken a lingering fast
With those who had fallen for that night's repast.
And Alp knew, by the turbans that rolled on the sand,
The foremost of these were the best of his band:
Crimson and green were the shawls of their wear,
And each scalp had a single long tuft of hair,
All the rest was shaven and bare.
The scalps were in the wild dog's maw,
The hair was tangled round his jaw. . . .   (stanza 16)

This scene apparently originated in the sight of two dogs
gnawing a dead body under the walls of the Palace of the
Sultans in Constantinople, when Byron and Hobhouse had
left the comfort of their ship's cabin for an outing in the city.
Galt comments:

> This hideous picture is a striking instance of the uses to
> which imaginative power may turn the slightest hint, and of
> horror augmented till it reach that extreme point at which
> the ridiculous commences. The whole compass of English
> poetry affords no parallel to this passage. It even exceeds the
> celebrated catalogue of dreadful things on the sacramental
> table in Tam O'Shanter . . . The whole passage is fearfully
> distinct, and though its circumstances, as the poet himself
> says, 'sickening', is yet an amazing display of poetical power
> and high invention.'   (148)

On the other hand, Galt finds that although the descriptions in
the seraglio section of *Don Juan* 'abound in picturesque beauty,
they have not that air of truth and fact about them, which
render the pictures of Byron so generally valuable, independent of their poetical excellence.' The reason for this, in Galt's
view, is that these passages had to come entirely from
invention, the seraglio not being accessible beyond the courts
and official apartments. In consequence he finds 'a vagueness'

in these descriptions 'which has the effect of making them obscure, and even fantastical . . . his gorgeous description of the sultan's seraglio is like a versified passage of an Arabian Tale, while the imagery of Childe Harold's visit to Ali Pashaw, has all the freshness and life of an actual scene' (150-51). One could argue that the impression of the 'obscure' and 'fantastical' in the seraglio section of Don Juan is in keeping with Juan's own sense of mystery with regard to his destination and its purpose, and with the expectations which his author wishes to arouse in his readers. It is interesting, however, that Galt's views are very much in line with his own practice as novelist. He insisted that Annals of the Parish and The Provost were 'theoretical histories'[10] not novels, and although they have the attributes of imaginative fiction they are in fact closely based on small town and parish life and records of their time. Like Byron's transformations of personal experience and observation in his poetry, they are artistic recreations which display a high order of imaginative activity.

Despite his view of the poet as a man of worldly affairs, Galt has little to say about Don Juan, which he calls 'a poetical novel' (263). He identifies the comedy of manners nature of the work, but seems strangely oblivious to Byron's serious attack on social hypocrisy: 'nor can it be said to inculcate any particular moral, or to do more than unmantle the decorum of society . . . affording ample opportunities to unveil the foibles and follies of all sorts of men – and women too' (263-4). He absolves it, however, from charges of immorality, remarking shrewdly that 'perhaps . . . there was more of prudery than of equity' in such criticism (266). He himself found it 'deficient as a true limning of the world, by showing man as if he were always ruled by one predominant appetite' (264). He appears to have been impervious to its sexual comedy.

In discussing Byron's love poetry, Galt draws attention to what he sees as the dichotomy between Byron's reputation as a womaniser, a reputation encouraged by Byron himself, and the lack of 'sensual images' in his love poetry. Instead Galt finds 'the icy metaphysical glitter of Byron's amorous allusions' (15). In his view, the poem 'She walks in beauty like the night' is 'a perfect example . . . of his bodiless admiration of beauty, and objectless enthusiasm of love,' and a poem where the 'simile' has become the 'the principal'. He continues: 'There is upon the subject of love, no doubt, much beautiful composition throughout his works; but not one line in all the thousands which shows a sexual feeling of female attraction – all is vague and passionless, save in the delicious rhythm of the verse' (16). This analysis applies to *Don Juan* also, where Galt notes that 'not even in the freest passages' has Byron associated beauty or love 'with sensual images' (15).

'She walks in beauty' is a fine lyric poem, but it is, as Galt's comments suggest, a poem of idealised, unattainable love, as elusive as Shelley's search for intellectual beauty. As such it is the antithesis of the kind of sexual relationships we find most often depicted in Byron's verse: worldly, uncommitted, often cynical, surprisingly deficient in sensual detail; the reader is led to supply this from his/her imagination or experience and in doing so, is drawn into the sexual conspiracy.

There is nothing in Byron's love scenes to compare with the eroticism and sensuousness of Porphyro's stolen meeting with Madeline in Keats's 'The Eve of St Agnes', which succeeds in being both idealised and of the tangible, everyday world. Byron's nearest approach to the depiction of an idealised yet fulfilled love is perhaps the Haidée episode in *Don Juan*, where the innocent love of the young lovers is at one with their natural, island environment, set apart from the corrupting influence of the 'civilised' world. Yet even here Byron's register is ambivalent and unstable, as if he fears to commit himself to his idyll. The early descriptions of the lovers' delight in each other and in their surroundings are frequently deflected in Byron's characteristic ironical manner: 'Well – Juan after bathing in the sea,/Came always back to coffee and Haidee' (II, 171), while as the tale proceeds, a sense of imminent tragedy begins to prevail over the initial flippancy. I find it impossible to integrate Haidée's ending into the predominant comedy-of-manners context of *Don Juan*: 'She died, but not alone; she held within/A second principle of life, which might/Have dawn'd a fair and sinless child of sin' (IV, 70) seems to introduce into the poem a note of genuine human tragedy and unfulfilled potentiality which is foreign to the way in which Byron more

typically chooses to put forward his view of the human
condition, and in consequence one cannot be drawn into the
comedy of Juan's activities in quite the same way as before the
Haidée interlude. A willing suspension of judgement has been
disturbed and cannot easily be restored.

If Galt has little to say about *Don Juan*, then he says even less
about *The Vision of Judgment*. In his criticism of the poem he
shows himself to be a political conservative, and, like his own
Provost Pawkie, stout in the defence of monarchy and
government. He refers to 'the disgust which The Vision of
Judgment had produced' and gives his opinion that 'much
good could not be anticipated from a work which outraged the
loyal and decorous sentiments of the nation towards the
memory of George III' (270). As Galt seems to have missed the
social criticism in *Don Juan*, so he seems to have overlooked the
even stronger satirical element in *The Vision*, and is more than a
little guilty of hypocrisy in his comments on the poem. George
III had not been admired in life and Byron is certainly not
over-generous towards him in death. Yet his attack is directed
as much against the hypocrisy of the trappings of political
mourning by an ungrieving nation – 'Who cared about the
corpse? The funeral/Made the attraction, and the black the
woe' (stanza 10) – as it is against the inadequacies of the king.
Similarly his religious satire in the poem has as its target
human beings who remake God in their limited, worldly
image and make of His heaven an Establishment Club to
which only those who follow the Establishment way in politics
and religion will be admitted.

Galt did not consider Byron to be an atheist like Shelley. His
view was that Byron

> had but loose feelings in religion . . . with him religion was a
> sentiment, and the convictions of the understanding had
> nothing whatever to do with his creed . . . He reasoned on
> every topic by instinct, rather than by induction or any
> process of logic; and could never be so convinced of the truth
> or falsehood of an abstract proposition, as to feel it affect the
> current of his actions.   (281)

He reports discussions between Byron and Dr Kennedy, a
religious man who sought to convert the poet to orthodox

Christianity when he was in Cephalonia. While Byron may have to some extent been playing with the doctor, these reported conversations do reveal to us the Byron of the poetry and the Count Maddalo of Shelley's 'Julian and Maddalo', who rejected Julian's and his author's evolutionary optimism for the deterministic creed that things are as they are. According to Dr Kennedy, Byron put forward his belief in 'predestination . . . and in the depravity of the human heart in general, and of my own in particular.' He continued: 'Pre destination appears to me just; from my own reflection and experience, I am influenced in a way which is incompre hensible, and am led to do things which I never intended, (289-90). He departs from orthodox predestination, however, in his insistence that 'I cannot yield to your doctrine of the eternal duration of punishment' (292). This too is the attitude of the narrator of *The Vision of Judgment* who knows 'one may be damn'd/For hoping no one else may e'er be so' (stanza 14), and who in the end lets George III slip into Heaven during the tumult aroused by the 'grand heroics' of Southey's poem of praise (stanza 103).

Byron's Calvinistic leanings in religion bring us to an aspect of his life and work which Galt surprisingly does not develop in his biography: Byron's dual Scottish and English ancestry, and the effect on his personality and poetry of his spending the formative years of childhood in Aberdeenshire. In the essay 'Byron', T. S. Eliot draws attention to what he considers Byron's un-Englishness, finding in 'his delight in posing as a damned creature', his satirical 'flyting' – a mode foreign to English literature but an attribute of the Scottish tradition – and his particular way with the English language an apartness from the English tradition and its context: 'for what Byron understands and dislikes about English society,' comments Eliot, 'is very much what an intelligent foreigner . . . would understand and dislike.'[11]

Galt pre-dated Eliot in drawing attention to Byron's apart ness from English traditions. Assessing Byron's achievement at the end of his biography, he comments on 'a great similarity' which 'runs through every thing that has come from the poet's pen; but it is a family resemblance, the progeny are all like one

another; but where', asks Galt, 'are those who are like them? I
know of no author in prose or rhyme, in the English language,
with whom Byron can be compared' (329). He finds that 'his
verse is often so harsh and his language so obscure . . . he
possessed not the instinct requisite to guide him in the selection
of the things necessary to the inspiration of delight.' And
finally Galt thought that Byron lacked 'a tuneful voice' (328).

All this suggests a writer who has anticipated Edwin Muir's
twentieth-century injunction to Scottish writers to *adopt* the
English language and tradition, rather than a poet who is at
home in English. Although Galt ascribes the 'conception of the
dark and guilty beings which he delighted to describe' to
Byron's 'mother's traditions of her ancestors' (21), unfortunately he does not develop the comment in the context of the
nature of these traditions and their distinctiveness from those
of England. He was aware of the inhibiting effect of the
'translation' procedures forced by public taste upon Scots-
speaking authors,[12] yet Galt's own work shows little of the
stress arising from the sense of a divided culture which we find
in Burns and Scott, for example. He seems on the whole to
have accepted his role as a North British writer, and to have
exploited successfully in his best work the linguistic potentiali-
ties of the two traditions. In turn, he ignores the possible
influence of the cultural divide in his discussions of Byron's
personality and poetic achievement.

Although Byron himself affects a longing for the 'Highland
cave' and 'dusky wild' of his childhood in the early poem 'I
would I were a careless child', and rejects 'the cumbrous pomp
of Saxon pride', this poem is something of an exercise in
rhetoric and role-playing which may well have taken its
starting- point from Coleridge's 'To the River Otter', with its
similar theme and final line: 'Ah! that once more I were a
careless child!' (Indeed, Galt – who himself had a brush with
Byron over possible plagiarism - tells us in the biography that it
was 'an early trick of his Lordship to filch good things' (183-4).)
On the whole, Byron appears to have accepted willingly his
transformation from penniless, if honourably descended,
Scotsman to English lord. It is noticeable that his satiric reply to
the criticism of the *Edinburgh Review* was entitled '*English* Bards

and Scotch Reviewers' (my emphasis). He does not draw on the Scots language which must have been part of his childhood background. Nor does he draw on Scottish themes, nor, consciously, on the Scottish literary tradition in his work. While one recognises the Calvinist in Byron's deterministic philosophy and also, perhaps, in his early alienated heroes, on the whole Byron's Calvinism does not lead to the censorious- ness associated with Scotland's reformed religion, but rather to a rejection of idealistic attempts to change human nature, and a comedy based on the acceptance of things as they are.

In addition, one does not find in Byron that ability to move easily from the everyday, domestic detail to the metaphysical or the conceptual which is a recurring feature in Scottish literature. Byron's apostrophe to freedom in Canto IV of *Childe Harold* – 'Yet Freedom! yet thy banner, torn, but flying,/ Streams like the thunder-storm *against* the wind' (stanza 98) – is a splendid rhetorical piece, but for me it remains mere rhetoric when constrasted with the freedom passage from John Barbour's *The Brus* which translates the idealistic concept into the conditions of everyday living.

On the other hand, as Galt and Eliot have pointed out, there are elements in Byron's poetry which do not fit easily into English literature. His particular form of satire with its extravagant moods, its wild lurches from urbane wit and irony to grotesque and often spiteful comic characterisation, brings to mind the Scottish tradition, as do his guilt-ridden heroes and his deterministic philosophy of existence. The wonder of the Alps and the mountains of Switzerland conjures up for Byron not a confirmation of the existence and power of God, as for Coleridge, nor the human mind's potential, as for Shelley. Standing at the foot of the Jungfrau, he watches the mountain torrent 'curving over the rock, like the tail of the white horse streaming in the wind just as might be conceived would be that of the pale horse in which Death is mounted in the Apocaly- pse' (quoted by Galt, 213). This seems a very Scottish response and image. He saw himself as Scott's heir: 'Sir Walter reign'd before me' (*Don Juan*, XI, 57). The Spenserian stanza he borrowed for *Childe Harold* came not directly from his knowledge of *The Faerie Queene*, but through the mediation of

the Scottish writers James Thomson and James Beattie, while
the *ottava rima* form first used in *Beppo* and which he made so
much his own in *Don Juan* and *The Vision of Judgment* came from
the Italian Pulci.

Although he claimed Pope as one of his masters, a comparison of Byron's couplets and satiric verse forms with the poetry
of Pope shows a formal unsettledness which patterns the lack
of a stable centre for his philosophical and moral perspectives.
Pope's couplets are formally and conceptually balanced. Even
when, like Byron, he is building up to a climax by an
accumulation of detailed effects, each stage has its own witty
or ironic point to make in addition to its apposite contribution
to the metaphor of the whole, as in this brief excerpt from the
description of the life cycle of Dullness in *The Dunciad*:

> Here she beholds the chaos dark and deep
> Where nameless Somethings in their causes sleep,
> Till Genial Jacob, or a warm Third day,
> Call forth each mass, a Poem, or a Play:
> How hints, like spawn, scarce quick in embryo lie,
> How new-born nonsense first is caught to cry,
> Maggots half-form'd in rhyme exactly meet,
> And learn to crawl upon poetic feet . . . (I, 55-62)

Byron, on the other hand, in *his* attack on what seems to him to
be literary dullness, does not succeed in achieving such
consistent conceptual, rhythmic and rhyming patterning:

> Bob Southey! You're a poet – Poet-laureate,
>   And representative of all the race;
> Although 'tis true that you turn'd out a Tory at
>   Last, – yours has lately been a common case;
> And now my Epic Renegade! what are ye at?
>   With all the Lakers, in and out of place?
> A nest of tuneful persons, to my eye
>   Like 'four and twenty Blackbirds in a pye . . .'
>   (*Don Juan*, Dedication)

Yet it would be unsafe to diagnose this more awkward verse as
stemming from a Scotsman's lack of identity with the English
language and tradition. It could as readily relate to the conflict

between the more formal verse conventions of an earlier period and the new, freer movement in ideas and syntax which one associaties with Romantic poetry. One of the hallmarks of Wordsworth's poetry is his ability to use blank verse as a conversational, reflective, meditative medium which enables his thoughts to flow forwards and backwards freely from line to line, turning, continuing, stopping where he will. Despite Byron's dislike of Wordsworth's poetic methods, his best verse also has this flexible immediacy, but it can often seem in conflict with the restrictions imposed by a tighter verse and rhyming pattern.

In the essay 'Byron as a Scottish Poet', the Scottish poet and critic Tom Scott puts forward a seductive case for Byron's membership of the Scottish tradition by translating the opening of *Beppo* into the kind of light Scots often used by Burns and MacDiarmid:

> It's kent, at least it sould be, that thurchoot
>   Aa countries o the Catholic persuasion,
> Some weeks afore Shrove Tuesday comes aboot,
>   The folk aa tak their fill o recreation,
> An buy repentance, ere they grouw devoot,
>   Houevir hiech their rank, or laich their station,
> Wi fiddlin, feastin, dancin, drinkin, maskin,
> An ither things that may be had for askin.[13]

Verse form apart, this does seem to sit happily alongside Burns's 'Holy Fair', while that 'an the mair murkily the better' in the stanza which follows the above reminds one of MacDiarmid's similar ironic use of parenthetical comments as, for example, in his 'an no' for guid' in the poem 'Lourd on my hert.'[14] On the other hand, Byron's *Beppo* seems to me to read equally well in its original English form – surely an almost unique achievement for any Scottish or English poet. The difference seems to be one of tone. Perhaps because of the characteristics of the Scots language, the narrator of Tom Scott's *Beppo* appears to be speaking from the *inside*. One expects him to go on to be part of the reveller's tale to be told and to draw the reader into the revelry with him. The English narrator, on the other hand, while uncensorious, even approving of the marital goings-on, remains an observer, keeping an aristocratic distance from the happenings, even while being entertained by them. In general, Byron's links with the Scottish tradition seem to be more implicit, related to sensibility and cast of mind, rather than overtly literary in nature.

The latter part of Galt's biography of Byron is inevitably based not on first-hand experience but on the reminiscences of others and on Byron's own journals. It appears that the two men fell out in 1813, the year of Galt's marriage and of Byron's continuing triumphs after the publication of the first two cantos of *Childe Harold*. Galt says little about the quarrel, leaving it to be assumed that marriage had put an end to his bachelor travels and acquaintanceship with Byron. Byron is reported by Lady Blessington as speaking admiringly of Galt in later years and regretting that he had taken 'no pains to cultivate his acquaintance further than I should with any common-place person, which he was not.'[15]

Galt's biography of Byron is certainly not commonplace. To the end he maintains the objectivity, percipience and unmalicious irony which is characteristic of his portrait. He views Byron's transformation from portrayer of heroes to man of action with some foreboding, a foreboding justified by the tragic events of Missolonghi. Galt's is necessarily a fragmentary biography, but it remains one of the fairest and most perceptive accounts of Byron and his work. As with Provost Pawkie, Galt has done well by his lord – and himself.

NOTES

1. Lord Byron, *Don Juan* Canto X, stanza 17.
2. John Galt, *The Life of Lord Byron* (London, 1830), 43. Page numbers for subsequent quotations from Galt's *Life* will be given in parentheses in the text.
3. *Lady Blessington's Conversations of Lord Byron*, ed. with introduction and notes by Ernest J. Lovell (1969), 146.
4. Ibid.
5. John Galt, *Annals of the Parish* (1821; Edinburgh: Mercat Press, 1980), 27.

6. Ibid., 27–8.
7. Ibid., 27.
8. William Wordsworth, Preface to *Lyrical Ballads*.
9. Alexander Pope, *Essay on Man*, Epistle II, 1–2.
10. John Galt, *Autobiography* (1833), II, 155–6.
11. T. S. Eliot, 'Byron', *English Romantic Poets: Modern Essays in Criticism*, ed. M. H. Abrams (1975), 262, 273.
12. See John Galt, 'Biographical Sketch of John Wilson', *Scottish Descriptive Poems*, ed. J. Leyden (1803), 14.
13. Tom Scott, 'Byron as a Scottish Poet', *Byron: Wrath and Rhyme*, ed. Alan Bold (1983), 29.
14. Hugh MacDiarmid, *To Circumjack Cencrastus, Complete Poems 1920–1976* (1978), 204.
15. *Blessington*, 146.

Lord Byron and Lord Elgin

DOUGLAS DUNN

Byron's encounter with the activities of Lord Elgin witnesses an episode in Byron's European and revolutionary mentality. It was political as well as poetic. Extreme, unorthodox and original, it shows Byron out of step with his times and far in advance of conventional opinion. It is an incident in Byron's work that called forth both satire and hortatory lyricism. Satire is more than poetry in its bad mood. Byron's satire can, at times, look like vindictive posturing, waves of sheer tantrum whose distempers preclude the sublime. Satire is poetry when it has decided on action and on the practical, and in the work of a poet as restless, itinerant and topical as Byron, it reaches beyond routine discourtesy and insult as if intent on an effective intervention. Although perhaps thinned out by the action of time, the values of Augustan satire survived in Byron's instinctive repertoire; they co-existed with the new melancholy his poetry invented, and with his libertarian hope and determination. Together these three sources of feeling and style characterized the poetry that was to have such a devasting effect on the literature of Europe, reflected in its music, opera, drama, painting and sculpture in the reactionary aftermath of Napoleon's defeat. As poetry, it is a fiery and elusive phenomenon: sometimes agonized, sometimes elegiac, sometimes languid, radical, republican or loud in its revolutionary encouragement, or Napoleonic, combative, soaring and inspired.

Thomas Bruce, seventh Earl of Elgin and eleventh Earl of Kincardine, was born in July 1766. He was therefore twenty-one years older than Byron. His father died in 1771 and Thomas Bruce's elder brother William became the sixth Earl. He died only two months later so that Thomas Bruce became

seventh Earl rather sooner than anyone had bargained for.
Like Byron, he was half-a-Scot: his mother was the daughter of
a London banker. Money and heiresses figure in Elgin's story
almost as much as in Byron's. While Byron could find
excitement in the Gordon history of his mother's side, Elgin
could point with satsifaction to a Bruce ancestry which had
provided a Scottish dynasty. Like Byron, he was at Harrow
school, though not for long, being transferred quickly to
Westminster. Subsequently, Elgin studied at St Andrews, and
then in Paris. Whatever else he might have been, he was far
from the half-witted archaeological impresario and shipping-
agent made out by his legion of detractors.

He opted for a military career in 1785. For a time he served as
an ensign in the Foot Guards, then after what looks like rapid
promotion, he commanded a regiment that he raised himself,
the Elgin Highland Fencibles. He was lieutenant-colonel by
the age of twenty-nine, and, by the time of his death, a
major-general. We cannot be sure of it, but senior military rank
before the age of thirty suggests a certain degree of competence.

Opportunities for a military career in Elgin's lifetime could
hardly be said to have been lacking. Yet he never saw active
service. His health was uncertain. He was a martyr to
rheumatism. A political and diplomatic career must therefore
have looked like an answer to a young man as ambitious as
Elgin appears to have been, or who at least considered himself
serviceable. He could have chosen the life of many Scottish
aristocrats, and done nothing.

At the age of twenty-four, in 1790, he approached Henry
Dundas whose manipulative and not entirely benign political
genius dominated Scottish public life. In those days Scotland
was served in the House of Lords by sixteen representative
peers. To get there, a Scottish aristocrat had to be elected,
which meant substantially that he required Dundas to appoint
him. Elgin achieved this, perhaps as a stepping stone to more
active work: at any rate, during the seventeen years that Elgin
held his seat he was abroad for most of them. It suggests, too,
that Elgin was ambitious and that his political views were
predictably those of his class. A year later he was appointed to

the Embassy to the Emperor Leopold II. From Envoy Extraordinary in Vienna, he went in the same capacity to Brussels, and after that to Berlin, at times rushing back to London to occupy his seat in the House of Lords where his contributions continued to recommend him to the government party. Serious European business was afoot in the 1790s, and Elgin must have been considered capable as well as politically and personally suitable. Nothing, so far, suggests that he was a fool. In the 1790s Elgin also instigated costly improvements to his house, Broomhall in Fife near Dunfermline. His mother pointed out the extravagance of her son's plans. 'Considering your Taste and style of living a prodigious House will be a monstrous burden,' she wrote. Not long after, Elgin married Mary Nisbet of Dirleton. Her family was worth something in the region of £18,000 a year, a lot more than Elgin's estates produced – £2000 a year seems the likeliest assessment of Elgin's independent wealth. No doubt it mattered that the future Lady Elgin was lively and good-looking. Elgin himself seems to have been dull, conscientious and prone to pomposity and stiffness. What also mattered were the future Lady Elgin's expectations. Alterations to Broomhall had made it necessary for Elgin to borrow heavily, and as well as an heiress he needed for the shorter term a prestigious and well-remunerated appointment. His selection as Ambassador Extraordinary and Minister Plenipotentiary to the Sublime Porte of Selim III, at a salary pf £6000 a year plus expenses, must therefore have looked almost as handsome as Mary Nisbet and perhaps as sublime as the Porte. It also represented promotion, and yet another sign that Elgin was considered a useful man to have in a diplomatically tricky and potentially significant corner of the world, already penetrated by French influence.

Before the recently married couple set off for Turkey, it was suggested to Elgin by Thomas Harrison, Elgin's dilatory architect at Broomhall, who was soon to be sacked, that his ambassadorship presented a golden opportunity for introducing to Britain authentic materials for the study of classical architecture and art. Harrison appears to have suggested the

making of accurate drawings, plaster casts, mouldings, mea-
surements and other reproductive and survey work, some of it
of an artistic nature, carried out on the spot, and with
systematic expertise. To some extent it would duplicate work
already published, and this was the reason given by Greville,
the Foreign Secretary, for refusing Elgin government funds for
the purpose.

Elgin committed himself to the idea of improving public
taste and appreciation of the arts, but it seems proper to
suggest that public taste might have held less appeal for Elgin
than the means through which he could make a name for
himself in a field of endeavour that could earn him the British
peerage he desired. No one, least of all Elgin himself, had in
mind the physical dismemberment of architectural sculptures
from the Parthenon and their shipment to Britain.

To fulfil this self-chosen, unofficial but enthusiastic part of
his mission, for which the government refused to pay, Elgin
interviewed a number of British artists. J. M. W. Turner was
one, but he asked for too much, and insisted also on keeping
his drawings and paintings, which failed to suit Elgin's pocket
and possessiveness. Thomas Girtin and William Daniell also
applied. It was *en route* to Turkey, however, at Sicily, that Elgin
met his artist, Lusieri – later a friend of Byron's when he visited
Greece a decade later. Lusieri was recommended by Sir
William Hamilton, husband of Emma, the Lady Hamilton of
Nelsonian fame. He was a connoisseur and antiquarian whose
collections had inspired Josiah Wedgewood and English
pottery. Also employed was Theodor or Fydor Ivanovich, a
colourful drunkard of obscure, exotic origins, probably a
Kalmuck or Tartar. Given that Lusieri was talented but
incorrigibly lazy (as well as loyal), and that the Kalmuk Fydor
was seldom sober enough to do what was required at the
requisite tempo, Elgin looks to have been courted by bad luck
from the start. Other employees turned out to be unreliable
and even treacherous. Drawings, Lusieri's responsibility, and
engravings, the Kalmuk's function, never materialized in a
state other than promised or unfinished.

As part of the Ottoman Empire in Europe, Greece had
stagnated into a condition of wearied resignation and cynical

survival. Athens was described by John Galt in *Letters from the Levant* (1813) as like several villages pressed into one with a population of around 10,000 people. It was a backwater, scraping into the top fifty of the towns of European Turkey. There was a Turkish garrison as well as a mosque on the Acropolis. A little over a hundred years before, Venetian artillery had devastated the Parthenon, setting off the Turkish arsenals and magazines. Ruthless as the Turks could be, the Greeks preferred them to the Venetians and their mercenary hirelings. In the past the Turks had taken boys for the corps of Janissaries, normally one per family, subjecting them to a thorough military and religious education. As in Bosnia and elsewhere in Turkish Europe, these professional soldiers of Christian origin rose to positions of high rank in the Empire. Young women were enlisted into the harems of officers and administrators. Able bodied men could end up pulling an oar in Turkish galleys; they could find themselves similarly hard-worked in Venetian vessels. Turkish capitation tax meant itself to be taken literally: pay up and you kept a head on your shoulders. But by the early nineteenth century tyranny was at the whim of local disdars and governors, while religious oppression had always been the exception rather than the rule. Most towns were sleepy and depressed; now and again life was animated by the visitation of brutality. Some districts were ungovernable, autonomous regions controlled by *klephts* or brigands whose armed bands were subsequently to form important units of the Greek revolutionary armies.

Elgin's employees were in Athens in August 1800, Lusieri arriving a little later, but Elgin was in Constantinople where he was engaged in countering the deviousness of the Levant Company and contending with its incumbents for whom Elgin's authority weakened their own. He was kept busy negotiating with the lethargic, ritualistic Turkish government, purchasing supplies for the British forces engaged in the war in Egypt. It was a responsibility which he seems to have discharged with fastidiousness, some of it at his own expense, always a risk, and perhaps even an expectation, borne by Britannic ambassadors of the time.

Reports from Athens also engrossed Elgin's attention. For

years the Turks had been casual pilferers of the Parthenon, usually for building materials, sometimes recycling statuary into mortar for new constructions. Whole temples had been blown up and cleared away. General Morosini's bombardiers of the 1680s had left their marks too, and some might even have been Scots, for the Venetians recruited Scottish troops for the wars of Candia (1649-1669). Also, the French were there, and their Consul had it in mind to remove choice examples of the classical artistry in stone, which was a potential threat to Elgin's quieter intentions as well as his career prospects. Parts had already been looted by sundry travellers and antiquarians. As work started on scale drawings and surveys, the local disdar laid a ban on any activity of the sort until a *firman* or note of authority could be produced from Constantinople.

Elgin pressed for this document with great vigour. Egypt, nominally a Turkish province, had been retaken; British favour ran high in Constantinople. There wasn't much that a Turkish government would deny a British ambassador. Bearing in mind the reports he had received from Athens – the French were after them; the Turks were disrespectful; the statuary seemed in danger – Elgin looked for, and got, the widest terms he could, or else Turkish vagueness conspired to provide the document he wanted. For an official instrument, the *firman* is remarkably unclear, leaving room for Elgin's interpretation – that he was at liberty to remove from the Parthenon what were decided to be of value to his philanthropic or self-regarding purposes. It seems never to have crossed his mind that a *firman* in strict terms preventing dismantlement and removal by the French or defacement by anyone else would have been more appropriate. That the French were at the time interned by the Turks might have led Elgin to believe that he had the chance to escalate their own greedy intentions, a patriotic opportunity for British gain which would enhance his prestige at home. It might look like the archaeological version of a victory. Other evidence suggests that if these thoughts ran through his mind, then so too did a more private avariciousness succeed them.

It was some time before Elgin set eyes on the objects of his goodwill towards art and Elgin, the statuary that was costing him a fortune in wages, tackle and gear. He visited Athens in the Spring of 1802 but only for as long as his duties permitted. His interest was intense, but distant; he seems to have acted in the matter like a grandee, behaving, perhaps, a little above his grandeur. On their return to England, the Elgins decided to travel much of the way through France. During their journey the war reopened, having been temporarily armisticed by the Treaty of Amiens in March 1802. They were interned. Napoleon, for whom the acquisition of European plunder was a serious business, held Elgin personally responsible for the fact that the Marbles were Elgin's and not his. The unfortunate Elgin was marooned in France for three years. He claimed that the French offered to release him in return for the Marbles. Elgin refused, and it forms a nice scene to imagine him weighing up his patriotic duty, his possible éclat in London, and his personal magnification, against an offer of being set at liberty. The invitation is credible when you consider the Napoleonic appetite for imperial aggrandisement.

It was a stroke of bad luck worsened by the terms of Elgin's subsequent parole, which tied him to an obligation to return to France whenever or if that might be demanded: it ruled out a continued diplomatic career for as long as the war continued. Lady Elgin added to his misfortunes. While in France she fell in love with another internee, Robert Ferguson of Raith, perhaps the original Raith' Rover, a Fife landowner of great wealth, a Fellow of the Royal Society and a Whig. There was a messy divorce – first a trial in London, and then another in Edinburgh in March 1808. Elgin came out of it with £10,000 in damages, useful money considering the almighty amounts disbursed for the sake of the Marbles, but it might have looked a pittance when contrasted with Mary Nisbet's inheritance, to say nothing of his growing debts and persistent creditors. He also had four children to look after.

Reports of Elgin's Parthenon scoop, added to the first sensational disclosures of his divorce in December 1807, which was widely publicized, made Elgin well known. It was a negative celebrity; scandal and an almost comically severe run of bad luck subtracted from the grateful acclaim that he might have believed he deserved. Among artists, what he had brought to Britain was welcomed, often ecstatically; its sculptural genius was upheld as exemplary in exactly the manner that Elgin must have hoped would be the case. Turner approved, as did Flaxman, Chantry, Benjamin West and many others, including Haydon, later the friend and encourager of Keats on whom the impact of the Parthenon sculptures was to play a significant part in the hastening and strengthening of his poetry. Fuseli, Nollekens, and Canova, the greatest sculptor of his day, were also more than impressed. Most of these artists had benfited from the Italian archaeological and restoration industry of the eighteenth century in which the Scottish artist and excavator Gavin Hamilton played a large part. What Elgin imported from Greece looked like the real thing to many in the best position to judge – heroic, inspiring, inestimable. The vigour and genius of Phidias and Praxiteles in three dimensions left British artists gaping in awe-struck wonder.

Dissenting voices contradicted this display of appreciation. Significantly, they came from connoisseurs and collectors, not artists. Richard Payne Knight was their leader, an arbiter of taste and a man whose envy and malice led him easily into doltishness. 'You have lost your labour, my lord Elgin,' he is reported as having said. 'Your marbles are overrated: they are not Greek. They are Roman of the time of Hadrian.' Perhaps only an English critic can be so wrong and still retain the power of spokesmanship. As a leading voice in the Society of Dilettanti, Knight's opinion carried weight with those in no position to judge for themselves or predisposed to welcome yet another stroke of bad luck in Elgin's mounting catalogue of calamities.

With all this going on it was inevitable that Byron should have become familiar with Lord Elgin and his deeds, his misfortune and financial embarrassments, his cuckolding, and the suspicion, now growing stronger, that Elgin had misused his ambassadorial trust in obtaining ambiguous rights from the Turkish government preparatory to his acquistion of the Marbles for himself, not for the nation. Byron's first satirical punch was struck in *English Bards and Scotch Reviewers*, which appeared in two editions in March and October 1809 before he departed on the tour that would take him to Greece. His

farewell peroration tells us what he will not do – he will not try
to make a name for himself by collecting lumps of antique
stone:

> Let ABERDEEN and ELGIN still pursue
> The shade of fame through regions of Virtu;
> Waste useless thousands on their Phidian freaks,
> Mis-shapen monuments and maimed antiques;
> And make their grand saloons a general mart
> For all the mutilated blocks of art . . .

Lord Aberdeen had been in Greece and returned with a few
stones – 'Athenian' Aberdeen he was called: he was not
entirely on Elgin's side in the controversy that had already
begun and was to continue to oppose him for several years
more, as Elgin attempted to off-load his burdensome collection
on the British government. Detectable in Byron's lines is a low
opinion of antiquities in a damaged condition and never mind
if they were sculpted by Phidias. His view was to be changed
when he experienced Greece and learned of the indigenous
value of antiquity to a suppressed nationality. 'The shade of
fame', too, hints at a topical hunch that Elgin's intentions had
less to do with art and were more concerned with limelight and
applause.

True to the sentiments of *English Bards and Scotch Reviewers*,
Byron was an unconventional voyager. With the rest of
Europe closed by warfare to young men on hedonistic or
educational journeys, Greece had become a favourite destination. High-born, classically educated young men were there
in numbers. Many held opinions on Elgin's removal of the
Marbles, rarely in his favour. Most, though, were happy to
thieve portable souvenirs of their own. Their estimates of
the contemporary Greeks were low. One traveller observed
that Arcadian shepherds had 'almost reverted to the
balenephageous state of their primitive ancestors.' That is,
they ate acorns. They were unworthy of the civilisation in
which these young visitors were schooled and of whose
language they knew more than the vast majority of Greeks
themselves. Contemptible, shabby and impoverished, the
inhabitants of a town like Athens offered a dispiriting contrast

to the glory represented by visible ruins. Where was their art, poetry, philosophy and power? Romaic, or *Demotiki*, modern Greek, was hardly in accord with the tongue of Homer and Euripides. Even more amusing or disgusting was that the natives called themselves *Romaioi*, or Romans, as they had done since the time of the eastern Roman empire and its Byzantine successor. Not even proper Christians, they were inferior, clearly, mere docile provincials of a backward despotism in which the only right they enjoyed was the right to be taxed. Lazy, servile, superstitious, greedy, untrustworthy, unwashed, degenerate and debased – to the comfortable nomads who descended on Greece, its people had nothing to recommend them.

'Plausible rascals', Byron called the Greeks. 'They are perhaps the most depraved and degraded people under the sun.' He liked them. A bi-sexual amorist, Byron's depravity was itself astounding, making up for what it lacked in cynicism with a voluptuary performance largely free of hypocrisy and erotic cant. He was aware of the political imperfections of the Greeks, but had the capacity of mind to notice that where the Greeks lived was Greece and that the long withering of Ottoman hegemony was worth a more active response than languid regret. He perceived how liberty and the dignity it bestows might transform native indolence. Whatever was contemptible about the inhabitants had been encouraged by generations of fatalism.

'Hobhouse rhymes and journalises. I stare and do nothing,' Byron reported. 'Do I look like one of these emasculated fogies?' he expostulated when invited to join a trip to nearby ruins. 'Let's have a swim.' But he was not idle. He began writing *Childe Harold's Pilgrimage* at Jannina in Epirus on 31 October 1809, finishing the second canto at Smyrna on the Turkish mainland on 28 March 1810. He began *The Curse of Minerva* in Athens; there is a likelihood that it was suggested by a poem of John Galt's called *The Atheniad* which Byron read in manuscript.

He wrote some shorter poems too, for example 'Maid of Athens, Ere We Part' or the translation of a 'Greek War Song by Rhigas Pheraios', in which he writes of 'The Turkish tyrant's yoke' and appeals to Sparta and Athens to rise from their slumber and defeatism. No other British traveller identified with a Greek cause; no other British traveller noticed that there was one. Lusieri, Elgin's artist-in-residence in Athens, was a frequent companion, guide and friend. Byron developed a sexual friendship with Nicolo Giraud, Lusieri's half-Greek brother-in-law. He saw at first hand Lusieri's dutiful defence of a second shipment of Marbles, holding off the covetous designs of Fauvel, who for years had been the French Consul in Athens and under instructions to lay his hands on as many treasures as possible with which to enrich the Louvre, the Musée Napoleon. With Lusieri and Nicolo Giraud, Byron sailed for Malta on board the ship *Hydra* which transported the second haul of Elgin's Marbles. Doubtless too, Byron picked up from Lusieri something close to a realistic picture of Lord Elgin's intentions.

At this point in the story we encounter an opportunistic near miss by John Galt, who was then in Athens. Aware of Elgin's shaky finances and that his bankers in Malta might easily refuse the necessary transaction, Galt instructed his agent in Malta to purchase the Marbles should Elgin's credit be refused. 'Here was a chance of the most exquisite relics of art in the world becoming mine,' Galt wrote in his *Autobiography* in 1833, 'and a speculation by the sale of them in London would realise a fortune,' he added, with a retrospective commercial sorrow not often associated with novelists. Had Elgin's credit not still looked good, the 'Galt Marbles' might now be on display beside Elgin's in the British Museum.

On his return to Britain, Byron offered *Childe Harold's Pilgrimage* to the publisher Miller, who turned it down on the grounds of its attack on Elgin. Miller was Elgin's publisher: he had issued Elgin's *Memorandum on the Subject of the Earl of Elgin's Pursuits in Greece* late in 1810. Byron was therefore unfamiliar with Elgin's version of events as well as his claim for reimbursement of expenses before the Marbles could be presented in the national collections.

Byron carried letters to Elgin from Lusieri, which he saw to it were delivered. In a letter dated 31 July 1810, to his former travelling companion, Hobhouse, Byron said,

Lord Elgin has been teazing to see me these last four days. I wrote to him, at his own request, all I knew about his robberies, and at last have written to say that it is my intention to publish (in Childe Harold) on that topic, I thought proper, since he insisted on seeing me, to give him notice that he might not have an opportunity of accusing me of double dealing afterwards.

As yet the hapless Elgin could have had no very sure idea of how much damage a Byronic intervention might wreak on his chequered fortunes. He was probably encouraged by the opinion of his former secretary, William Richard Hamilton, who believed that Byron's negative opinion would do Elgin's cause the world of good. Hamilton had prised the Rosetta Stone from French hands after their defeat in Egypt. That, too, is in the British Museum, where its presence seems strangely uncontroversial.

That was the closest Elgin and Byron came to meeting. Byron's mother died on 1 August, and his friend Matthews soon after. By 10 August he was writing again to Hobhouse: 'I am very lonely, and should think myself miserable were it not for a kind of hysterical merriment, which I can neither account for nor conquer.' Mourning, laughing and wining, Elgin and the Marbles were far from Byron's mind.

Canto II, the Greek Canto of *Childe Harold's Pilgrimage*, contains only one passage of satire and it deals with the pillage of the Parthenon. Understanding the Canto demands that we attend to its view of history. It is elegiac as well as lively in its incitements: it reads like a reprimand delivered against time. 'Ancient of days! august Athena! where,/Where are thy men of might? thy grand in soul?' Childe Harolde ruminates on the ruins of Greece. 'Is this the whole?' he asks. 'A school-boy's tale, the wonder of an hour!' Structural and rhetorical cunning hold Byron's stanzas to an insistent narrative travelogue in which the past is visited as much as the present, and the spirit as much as the fact:

> Look on its broken arch, its ruin'd wall,
> Its chambers desolate, and portals foul:
> Yes, this was once Ambition's airy hall,

The dome of Thought, the palace of the Soul:
Behold through each lack-lustre, eyeless hole,
The gay recess of Wisdom and of Wit
And Passion's host, that never brook'd control:
Can all, saint, sage, or sophist ever writ,
People this lonely tower, this tenement refit?

Trembling, questioning and elegiac, the mood continues,
half lament and half accusation, until by Stanza XI he courts
the topical and contemporary.

But who, of all the plunderers of yon fane
On high, where Pallas linger'd, loth to flee
The latest relic of her ancient reign;
The last, the worst, dull spoiler, who was he?
Blush, Caledonia! such thy son could be!
England! I joy no child he was of thine:
Thy free-born men should spare what once was free;
Yet they could violate each saddening shrine,
And bear these altars o'er the long-reluctant brine.

QUOD NON FECERUNT GOTI, HOC FECERUNT SCOTI, a
Latinate wag had chipped into a column on the Parthenon. But
Byron, like Elgin, was half-Scots. Why this gratuitous sally
against Elgin as a Scot when Englishmen had already proved
themselves adept at cultural burglary? It was convenient; it
spiced his detestation of Elgin with mischief directed against
Byron's maternal country. Conceivably, it was an act of
instinctive revenge for humiliations experienced in his childhood.

But most the modern Pict's ignoble boast,
To rive what Goth, and Turk, and Time hath spar'd:
Cold as the crags upon his native coast,
His mind as barren and his heart as hard,
Is he whose head conceiv'd, whose hand prepar'd,
Aught to displace Athena's poor remains:
Her sons too weak the sacred shrine to guard,
Yet felt some portion of their mother's pains,
And never knew, till then, the weight of Despot's chains.

Elgin's argument was that the Turks were careless, casual wreckers of the Parthenon, while the Greeks couldn't care less. Other Greeks, however, looked on the visible residue of previous civilisation as supports to revolutionary action, as declarations of independence reared in stone. Byron ignored French plans for the removal of the Marbles. 'Tell not the deed to blushing Europe's ears,' he wrote. Europe was not blushing; it was bleeding. French embarrassment stemmed from their failure to take the Marbles for Napoleon's gratification. Satire breezed over these complicating factors and introduced a vituperative note of opinion to the otherwise persuasive movement of poetry.

Before the notion of 'imperialism' was coined (it enters the language in the 1850s), Byron had perceived its meaning.

> The ocean queen, the free Britannia bears
> The last poor plunder from a bleeding land . . .

'I have some early prepossession in favour of Greece,' Byron wrote, 'and do not think the honour of England advanced by plunder, whether of India or Attica.' Elgin, as a diplomat, a soldier, and a man of high orthodox beliefs and ambitions, probably failed to understand the gist of Byron's complaint.

> Cold is the heart, fair Greece! that looks on thee,
> Nor feels as lovers o'er the dust they lov'd . . .

Byron chastises British scholars, travellers and gentlemen, satisfying their classical educations with insensitive sight-seeing. In the lyrical embrace of these lines there is a sense, too, of European culture regretted as disrespectful of a civilisation that contributed largely to its identity. It is part of Byron's lament for the cruelty of time and the ironic displacements of history that relegate whole civilisations to the status of memory, fragments and plundered monuments. In that context, his abusive treatment of Elgin acts as a trigger to the topical. 'Fair Greece! sad relic of departed worth!' he exclaims by Stanza LXXIII.

> Immortal, though no more! though fallen, great!
> Who now shall lead thy scatter'd children forth,
> And long accustom'd bondage uncreate?

'Spirit of Freedom!' he shouts, 'lost Liberty!' His verse is not only sung at a Romantic pitch, but it is practical; there is nothing inactive or beaten about Byron's history.

> For foreign arms and aid they fondly sigh,
> Nor solely dare encounter hostile rage,
> Or tear their name defil'd from Slavery's mournful page.

Ten years before the Greek wars of independence, Byron wrote like an astute, lyric propagandist, editorialising in song, the breathless volume of his incitements directed as much to the Greeks as anyone else:

> Hereditary bondsmen! know ye not
> Who would be free themselves must strike the blow?
> By their right arms the conquest must be wrought?
> Will Gaul or Muscovite redress ye? no!
> True, they may lay your proud despoilers low,
> But not for you will Freedom's altars flame.
> Shades of the Helots! triumph o'er your foe!
> Greece! change thy lords, thy state is still the same;
> Thy glorious day is o'er, but not thine years of shame.

When Byron woke up to find himself eating the breakfast of a celebrity, Elgin's rise from bed that same morning was to discover his notoriety even more widely distributed. As the years passed before June 1816 when the House of Commons decided to pay Elgin – by a margin of two votes out of one hundred and sixty-two votes cast – Byron's own notoriety had been disclosed in the scandal of his failed marriage. Rumours of sodomy and incest made it impossible for Byron to remain in England and after April 1816 he was never to return. It is just possible that Byron's scandal saved the day for Elgin when his case was debated by truculent parliamentarians. Elgin was voted £35,000. By then his debts incurred in bringing the Marbles to Britain amounted, plus interest, to £90,000 according to Elgin's own figures. A few pieces remain at Broomhall and at one time, in a moment of desperation, Elgin considered installing the entire collection there, although, earlier in Turkey, at the height of his enthusiasm, he seems to have intended his Parthenon swag solely to adorn his house.

Statements testifying to their beauty and importance cut very
little ice with the government. In those days artists enjoyed as
much prestige as tradesmen and their opinions were easily
discounted. It did not matter that Goethe, for instance,
decorated his house in Weimar with Haydon's drawings of
the statuary, believing that the works carried out under the
direction of Phidias proved what Goethe's aesthetics had come
to be. Later, it would count for little that Keats had been
inspired by the controversial statuary, not only in two sonnets,
but as his gifts grew and his imagination lived more with what
he had experienced of Greek art, in *Endymion*, 'Ode on a
Grecian Urn, and *Hyperion*.

Classicism in British art and architecture was already
running out of impetus. By 1830 a Gothic design was chosen
for the House of Parliament, much to Elgin's disgust. It
was left to the Scottish architect James 'Greek' Thomson
to bring the style to its most original achievement in this
country. Ironically, one of his finest buildings was Elgin Place
Congregational Church at 240 Bath Street in Glasgow. Calton
Hill Monument in Edinburgh, an unfinished attempt to
reconstruct the Parthenon, was undertaken at the suggestion
of Elgin. It was also a dream of the Scottish artist H.W.
Williams, who published two volumes of his Greek travels in
1820.

Byron's angriest attack on Elgin appeared in *The Curse of
Minerva*. A privately printed version was circulated in 1812 but
the complete poem remained unpublished until after Byron's
death. Augustan measures guide Byron's satire from one
immoderate sentiment to another: the impression is of rancour
and vindictiveness disciplined by the equity that lurks within
the balance of heroic couplets and antitheses. Iambic justice,
the drum roll of English tradition in its encounter with the
literature of antiquity, rallies to its assault, which will be
personal, and all the while the reasonableness of the verse
carries with it enough propriety and a sense of redress to
clothe Byron's bad temper with satirical privilege.

"Mortal!" ('twas thus she spake) "that blush of shame
Proclaims thee Briton, once a noble name;

First of the mighty, foremost of the free,
Now honoured *less* by all, and *least* by me:
Chief of thy foes shall Pallas still be found.
Seek'st thou the cause of loathing? – look around.
Lo! here, despite of war and wasting fire,
I saw successive tyrannies expire;
'Scap'd from the ravage of the Turk and Goth,
Thy country sends a spoiler worse than both.
Survey this vacant, violated fane;
Recount the relics torn that yet remain:
These Cecrops placed, *this* Pericles adorned,
That Adrian rear'd when drooping Science mourn'd.
What more I owe let Gratitude attest –
Know, Alaric and Elgin did the rest.
That all may learn from whence the plunderer came,
The insulted wall sustains his hated name:
For Elgin's fame thus grateful Pallas pleads,
Below, his name – above, behold his deeds!
Be ever hailed with equal honour here
The Gothic monarch and the Pictish peer:
Arms gave the first his right, the last had none,
But basely stole what less barbarians won.
So when the Lion quits his full repast,
Next prowls the Wolf, the filthy Jackall last:
Flesh, limbs, and blood the former make their own,
The last poor brute securely gnaws the bone.
Yet still the Gods are just, and crimes are crost:
See here what Elgin won, and what he lost!
Another name with *his* pollutes my shrine:
Behold where Dian's beams disdain to shine!
Some retribution still might Pallas claim,
When Venus half-avenged Minerva's shame.''

Elgin's 'crime' is roundly cursed in the passage: Minerva
claims the intervention of Venus on her behalf, her half-
vengeance referring to Mary, Lady Elgin, by then Elgin's
ex-wife. Supernatural properties, Britain's alleged shame, or a
pairing like 'Alaric and Elgin' contrasted with Pericles and
Hadrian, or the wolf and the jackal, conspire to demean Elgin

as a barbarian worse than a Goth, and to dignify Byron's
animosity as the justice of the Gods. Byron's satirical tactics are
faultless: high-flown historical purpose transacts with squalid
bile, and neither seems to mock the other.

> She ceas'd awhile, and thus I dared reply,
> To soothe the vengeance kindling in her eye:
> 'Daughter of Jove! In Britain's injur'd name,
> A true-born Briton may the deed disclaim.
> Frown not on England; England owns him not:
> Athena! no; thy plunderer was a Scot.
> Ask'st thou the difference? From fair Phyle's towers
> Survey Boeotia; – Caledonia's ours.
> And well I know within that bastard land
> Hath Wisdom's goddess never held command:
> A barren soil, where Nature's germs, confin'd
> To stern sterility can stint the mind;
> Whose thistle well betrays the niggard earth,
> Emblem of all to whom the land gives birth;
> Each genial influence nurtur'd to resist,
> A land of meanness, sophistry and mist:
> Each breeze from foggy mount and marshy plain
> Dilutes with drivel every drizzly brain,
> Till burst at length each wat'ry head o'erflows,
> Foul as their soil, and frigid as their snows:
> Then thousand schemes of petulance and pride
> Despatch her scheming children far and wide;
> Some East, some West, some – every where but North,
> In quest of lawless gain, they issue forth
> And thus – accursed be the day and year!
> She sent a Pict to play the felon here.'

Elgin's felonious connoisseurship touched Byron on a raw
nerve. Before he went to Greece he was already contemptuous
of 'emasculated fogies', the geriatric castrati of country-house
antiquarianism. Once there, he noticed that the removal of relics
robbed a place of its poetry. In his 'Letter on the Rev. W. L.
Bowles's Strictures on the Life and Writings of Pope', he wrote:
> . . . to whatever spot of earth these ruins were transported, if
> they were *capable* of transportation, like the obelisk, and the

sphinx, and the Memnon's head, *there* they would still exist in the perfection of their beauty, and in the pride of their poetry. I opposed, and ever will oppose, the robbery of ruins from Athens, to instruct the English in sculpture; but why did I do so? The *ruins* are as poetical in Piccadilly as they were in the Parthenon; but the Parthenon and its rock are less so without them. Such is the poetry of art.

It was a theft, too, that by Byron's lights insulted the cause of Greek independence and illustrated the careless manner of British superiority and self-interest. Elgin's nationality – as a nobleman whose ambitions were directed chiefly at British preferment, it is tempting to see his Scottishness as border-line – was a convenient catalyst to Byron's own ambiguous, marginal Scottishness, which he disliked and distrusted except when it suited him to appear otherwise. Yet in such lines as,

> Each genial influence nurtured to resist;
> A land of meanness, sophistry and mist . . .

Byron was perhaps exercising more Scottishness than he knew. Their exaggeration is undeniable, but they summarize what many Scottish writers have perceived and contested, as do these lines:

> Yet Caledonia claims same native worth,
> And dull Boeotia gave a Pindar birth;
> So may her few, the letter'd and the brave,
> Bound to no clime and victors of the grave,
> Shake off the sordid dust of such a land,
> And shine like children of a happier strand;
> As once, of yore, in some obnoxious place,
> Ten names (if found) have saved a wretched race.

Minerva's curse then falls on the head of the already ruined Elgin, referring, in all likelihood and with considerable cruelty, to Elgin's epileptic son:

> "First on the head of him who did this deed
> My curse shall light – on him and all his seed:
> Without one spark of intellectual fire,
> Be all the sons as senseless as the sire."

Not even Byron and Minerva, however, could prevent Elgin's son, the eighth Earl of Elgin, from a career of great integrity, his diplomacy taking him to Jamaica, Canada, China and Japan, and finally as Viceroy to India. In case such an event might happen, Byron covered himself:

> If one with wit the parent brood disgrace,
> Believe him bastard of a brighter race:
> Still with his hireling artists let him prate,
> And Folly's praise repay for Wisdom's hate;
> Long of their Patron's gusto let them tell,
> Whose noblest, *native* gusto is – to sell:
> To sell, and make – may Shame record the day,
> The State receiver of his pilfer'd prey . . .

True-born Briton or not, not even Byron could get out of that one – although by a mere two votes, Westminster appropriated the Marbles, and, at least officially if not historically, Elgin was cleared of wrong-doing and of crossing the line between ambassadorship and entrepreneurial interests in art and architecture.

Elgin remarried. His second wife, Elizabeth Oswald of Dunnikeir in Fife, bore eight children to add to the four presented by Mary Nisbet. £18,000 of the expenses coughed up by the government were immediately transferred to creditors who had craftily assigned their requirements in advance to the government itself. Elgin's request to the government was limited to the recovery of his costs; he did not add to them an estimate of their value. 'I have been activated by no motives of private emolument,' he declared, 'nor deterred from doing what I felt to be a substantial good, by considerations of personal risk, or the fear of calumnious misrepresentations.'

Elgin's statement is tinged with retrospective self-justification. Fear of French depredations, an ambiguous *firman* produced at a moment when British favour ran high with the Turkish government, opened up to Elgin an opportunity in which his original, benign intentions took second place to personal aggrandizement. Enough of this was known at the time for Byron to feel sure of his opinions, and for parliament to come to such a close decision. It looks possible that governmental propriety and face-saving came to Elgin's partial rescue, and that parliamentary criticism gave it a close run.

Elgin's petitions to the government and public opinion must have appeared tedious and incessant, the desperation of a debtor, the turn-around of a man who thought he had trumped his fortunes with a stunt of artistic, patriotic daring, selflessness disguising private, acquisitive pride. Onlookers would have been divided between the comedy of the episode as it afflicted Elgin, and its offensiveness as it afflicted the public purse and Greek integrity. So many enemies in his life suggests that Elgin might have been an unpleasant man. After Constantinople he was not even much to look at: he lost most of his nose to an unidentified disease. His picture in the National Portrait Gallery shows him leaning self-confidently on his sword: his expression conveys pride and impatience, the hand on his hip suggests more than a hint of swagger and aristocratic disdain.

John Galt suggested to Byron that he might have overstepped the boundaries of satire. Byron replied, '& if you will prove to me that Ld. Elgin's *is* "the error of a liberal mind" the "Muse" shall forthwith eat her own words although they choak her – & me into the bargain.'

Elgin signed an early petition in favour of the Greek nationalists, as did Byron. Unlike Byron he did not join the Greek Committee, an organization of men and women later to be known as the Philhellenes. British policy was discouraging, and Elgin, still hopeful of a British peerage – he had been returned as a representative Scottish peer in 1820 – would in all likelihood have imitated it. Castlereagh and Wellington, for instance, were anti-Greek.

Among the volunteers who served with the Greek land and naval forces, the proportion of Irish and Scots was noticeably high. Colonel C. M. Woodhouse, an authority on this subject, has described it as a surrogate of Scottish and Irish nationalism. Whatever Byron might have thought of Caledonia, its libertarians, adventurers and freebooters were not slow to enlist in a fight for freedom, as many saw it, or an opportunity

for military hedonism, as it was seen by others. Admiral Lord
Cochrane harnessed Greek seamanship to brilliant effect.
Thomas Gordon of Cairness rose to the rank of General in the
Greek armies. One or two even changed sides, sickened by
Greek atrocities, only to be sickened yet again by Turkish
brutality.

Unwittingly, Elgin, at Byron's tender mercy, contributed
towards convictions and events distant from his own mind
and intentions. History is never simple. Kapodistrias, for
example, a leader of the Greek movement, had helped the Tsar
draw up the terms of the Holy Alliance. Elgin's activities
roused Byron's animosity and helped Byron to identify his
sympathies, lending a topical note to *Childe Harold's Pilgrimage*
(Elgin is the only living person mentioned) that braced his
verse with an incident a British public could hang on to. The
poem contributed to the beliefs of a generation, disposing
many towards a favourable view of the struggle that led to the
first new nation state of nineteenth-century Europe.

The controversy for which Elgin must be held responsible is
still unresolved. In his book of Greek travels, Hobhouse
reported:

> I cannot forbear mentioning a singular speech of a learned
> Greek of Ionnina who said to me, "You English are carrying
> off the works of the Greeks, our forefathers – preserve them
> well – we Greeks will come and redemand them."

They have been asking for their return ever since the 1830s.
Successive British administrations have refused to countenance the idea. As Scots we have an interest in encouraging
the restitution of the Parthenon sculptures, and in disproving
the Byronic assessment of a nationality that contributed to
Greek nationhood. It would be a decision that expressed
coincidentally that we cared for our own culturally depleted
country.

Byron: An Edinburgh Re-Review

JON CURT

In the early years of the nineteenth century, the recently founded *Edinburgh Review* was not primarily a literary journal. Instead, the majority of the contributors concerned themselves with the political and economic developments of the day – both words having much broader implications then than they do now. Nevertheless, in the interests of being a well-rounded periodical, some attention had to be given to advances in the literary field, although this was usually regarded as an opportunity to deride such respected and established poets as Wordsworth and Coleridge. Only Scott could reasonably expect to treated with the sort of courtesy and consideration most writers feel they deserve. In this way, *The Edinburgh Review* had already gained the reputation of savaging most of the literature that came its way, prompting Shelley to say some years later 'In my opinion, the *Edinburgh Review* is as well qualified to judge the merits of a poet, as Homer would have been to write a commentary on the Newtonian System.'[1] Of course, Shelley had an axe to grind with most reviewers, but in the case of this particular journal there may be more than a germ of truth in his opinion. Given this intolerance of even the highly regarded authors of the day, how much more damning could it be when confronted with a small collection of verse, unpromisingly entitled *Hours of Idleness* and written, according to the title page, by 'George Gordon, Lord Byron, a Minor'? This, surely, was a lamb to the slaughter.

The actual review appeared in *The Edinburgh Review*, number XI, in January 1808, and was written, anonymously, by Henry Brougham, whose cultural preferences were well demonstrated two years later when he became an English Member of Parliament. As a piece of criticism, it is essentially a highly sarcastic attack on Byron's false modesty about publishing the poems at all, as expressed in the 'Preface'. Indeed, Brougham consistently ignores the verse and quotes so extensively from what is, after all, a short preface, that Byron can be forgiven for feeling that the review was more of an attack on his person than his poetry. The last paragraph is typical:

But whatever judgement may be passed on the poems of this noble minor, it seems we must take them as we find them, and be content, for they are the last we shall ever have from him. He is at best, he says, but an intruder in the groves of Parnassus; he never lived in a garret like thorough-bred poets; and 'though he once roved a careless mountaineer in the Highlands of Scotland', he has not of late enjoyed this advantage. Moreover, he expects no profit from his publication; and whether it succeeds or not, 'it is highly improbable from his situation and pursuits hereafter' that he should again condescend to become an author. Therefore, let us take what we get and be thankful. What right have we poor devils to be nice? We are well off to have got so much from a man of this lord's station, who does not live in a garret, but 'has the sway' of Newstead Abbey. Again, we say, let us be thankful; and with honest Sancho, bid God bless the giver nor look the gift horse in the mouth.[2]

It is hardly surprising that Byron felt this review so strongly, although to his credit, he hid his anger from all but his closest friends until such time as it could be profitably vented in the poem that was to become *English Bards and Scotch Reviewers*. With admirable resignation, he wrote to a friend, John Becher, on 26 February 1808:

. . . You know the System of the Edinburgh Gentlemen is universal attack, they praise none, and neither the public nor the author expects praise from them, it is however something to be noticed, as they profess to pass judgement only on works requiring public attention.

The next month, again to Becher, Byron is still presenting the front of a man determined to make the most of his bad luck: 'For my own part, these "paper bullets of the brain" have only taught me to stand fire; and as I have been lucky enough upon the whole, my repose and appetite are not discomposed'[3]

(28 March 1808). But on 27 February he had written to his lifelong friend, John Cam Hobhouse, in what we feel sure was a more honest tone: "As an author, I am cut to atoms by the E Review, it is just out and has completely demolished my little fabric of fame.'

Both sides of Byron's attitude to bad reviews – his own sensitivity and the swaggering bravado he assumed – can be seen in his reaction to the news of Keats's death. Not knowing the facts, he genuinely believed, for some time at any rate, that he had been slain by an unfavourable review in the *Quarterly*. Writing to John Murray, he says:

> You know very well that I did not approve of Keats's poetry, or principles of poetry . . . but as he is dead, – omit *all* that is said *about him* in any MSS of mine . . . I do not envy the man – who wrote the article – your review people have no more right to kill than any other foot pads. However – he who would die of an article in a review – would probably have died of something else equally trivial . . .[4]

Recollecting his first review in his journal five years later, Byron confesses to a feeling of anger and hints at the intriguing possibility that *English Bards and Scotch Reviewers* was actually started on the day the review was published:

> I remember the effect of the *first* Edinburgh Review on me. I heard of it six weeks before, – read it the day of its denunciation – dined and drank three bottles of claret, . . . neither ate nor slept the less, but, nevertheless, was not easy till I had vented my wrath and my rhyme, in the same pages against everything and every body.[5]

That 'wrath and rhyme' eventually found its way into the poem published in 1809, *English Bards and Scotch Reviewers*, in which Byron first found his satiric tone which, as he continued to hone and refine it, became the essence of his greatest poetry. In the 'Preface' to the poem, Byron makes explicit the targets of the satire:

> As to the *Edinburgh Reviewers*; it would, indeed, require a Hercules to crush the Hydra; but if the Author succeeds in merely 'bruising one of the heads of the serpent', though his own hand should suffer in the encounter, he will be amply satisfied.[6]

Ironically, the 'one head' he thought he was bruising – that of
Francis Jeffrey, who is addressed by name in the 'Postscript' to
the second edition, and the attack on whom occupies 101 lines
of the poem[7] – was not, as we have seen, the reviewer of *Hours
of Idleness*.

Exactly ten years after that first review, it was indeed Jeffrey
who reviewed *Beppo* in *The Edinburgh Review*, number XXIX,
February 1818. Of course, by then Byron was far and away the
most popular poet of the day, and was not to be mocked as
some 'noble minor'. Quite apart from the praise and admiration for the style of the poem, the review is characterised by the
uncertainty that Byron is actually the poet in question, since
Beppo was published anonymously and was Byron's first
attempt at a poem in the *ottava rima* stanza which he was to
make his own in the following years. Jeffrey, obviously with a
clear recollection of what happened the last time Byron
thought he had reviewed his poetry, squirms uncomfortably
through several pages before a closing paragraph in which he
fawns:

> We are not in the secret of this learned author's incognito;
> and at our distance from the metropolis, shall not expose
> ourselves by guessing. We cannot help thinking, however,
> that we have seen him before, and that 'We do not know that
> fine Roman hand'. At all events, we hope we shall see him
> again: and if he is not one of our old favourites, we are afraid
> we may be tempted to commit an infidelity on his account, –
> and let him supplant some of the less assiduous of the
> number.[8]

To point out the open contradiction between Brougham's
and Jeffrey's reviews is obvious: Brougham sighing his relief at
'the high improbability from his sitation and position hereafter, that he should again condescend to become an author',
compared to the rather sycophantic hope expressed by Jeffrey,
that 'we shall see him again . . . one of our old favourites',
but this is to do both reviewers an injustice. The fact remains
that *Beppo* is a much better poem than anything in *Hours of
Idleness*, and perhaps, when faced with yet another collection
of adolescent verses, penned by a self-confessed 'minor',
Brougham was right to concentrate his attack on the slightly

absurd posture of the young lord who so obviously wanted to be taken seriously.

Before leaving *The Edinburgh Review* behind, and moving on to the end of the nineteenth century, it is worthwhile pointing out that at no time in the years of its composition and publication did the *Review* attempt an assessment of *Don Juan*. Byron's plays were all considered – many at greater length than they deserved – but his *magnum opus* never figured in the pages of the illustrious journal. This may be insignificant, but one might speculate as to possible reasons for this apparent oversight: indifference to the work seems unlikely; fear of further reprisals for a hostile review, especially now that Byron and Jeffrey were the best of friends, seems unnecessarily cautious; which leaves the possibility that in this most decorous of European capitals, it might be best to pretend that evil Lord Byron's profligate poem did not exist at all.

Edinburgh figured once again in the forum of Byron criticism and commentary in 1896, when Professor George Saintsbury published his *History of Nineteenth Century Literature*, which, as the title suggests, purports to cover one hundred particularly productive years of writing in fewer than five hundred pages. Even the logistic constraints of such a project fail to explain why only five pages are devoted to Byron – and why those few comments should constitute the fullest consideration of the poet by the man who was certainly the greatest academic critic of his generation in Britain. This ignoring, or even ignorance, of Byron is not untypical of the late Victorians, who felt that he had too vulgar a style for his work to be what was then considered poetry of the first order.

Saintsbury begins with the standard comparison between Sir Walter Scott and Byron – Scott having been usurped as the most popular poet of the day by the scuccess of *Childe Harold's Pilgrimage* and Byron's subsequent Eastern Tales. Not surprisingly, Scott comes off best: 'Indeed, Scott, with all his indifference to a strictly academic correctness, never permitted himself the bad rhymes, the bad grammar, the slipshod phrase in which Byron unblushingly indulges.'[9] It was to be sixty years until another great Edinburgh professor, W. W. Robson, was to point out that Byron was the exponent of a technique, or lack of technique, which permitted him not only to tolerate second-rateness, but to elaborate it with gusto. As for Saintsbury's claim of bad grammar, it is interesting to place it alongside Byron's own defence of *Don Juan* in a letter to Douglas Kinnaird, where he writes: 'As to *Don Juan*, confess, confess – you dog, and be candid, – that it is the sublime of *that there* sort of writing – it may be bawdy, but is not good English? It may be profligate, but is it not the life, is it not the thing?' (26 October 1819).

Saintsbury then dwells on Byron's enormous popularity, and makes of this another strand of his argument – namely, that popularity on that sort of scale must equal vulgarity. Using this as his main premise, and with a gigantic leap, the logic of which hardly conceals its absurdity, he then dismisses the whole of continental Europe with a single sweep:

Is he a poetic star of the first magnitude, a poetic force of the first power at all? There may seem to be rashness, there may even seem to be puerile insolence and absurdity in denying or even doubting this in the face of such a European concert as has been described and admitted above. Yet the critical conscience admits of no transaction; and after all, as it was doubted by a great thinker whether nations might not go mad like individuals, I do not know why it should be regarded as impossible that continents should go mad like nations.[10]

Having accounted for those injudicious enough to actually *like* Byron's poetry, or those, like Goethe and others, who allowed themselves to be influenced by it, Saintsbury turns his attention, albeit very briefly, to the verse itself: 'His verse is to the greatest poetry what melodrama is to tragedy, what plaster is to marble, what pinchbeck is to gold.'[11]

It is tempting to treat Saintsbury as dismissively as he himself treats Byron, but that ignores the important possibility that he started reading Byron from the beginning, and worked his way through. To do this would mean starting with *Hours of Idleness*, which, as Brougham observed, is not high art in any shape or form. After that, the methodical reader is faced with the inconsistencies of *Childe Harold's Pilgrimage* and the relentless gothic egoism of the Eastern Tales. By the time one reaches the refreshing linguistic adventures of the *ottava rima* poems, one's palate may well have become so jaded as to miss their worth altogether. To be fair to Saintsbury, he has, like so many others, found himself with the wrong yardstick by which to measure Byron's later poems and has lapsed into some kind of moralistic disapproval. As we have seen, Byron maintained that *Don Juan* was 'the sublime of *that there* sort of writing', the '*that there*' being underlined to emphasise the point that this was something contemptuous of tradition and convention, at the same time as being linguistically legitimised by its use of colloquial language and expression. Saintsbury's problem with *Don Juan* was something to which Byron was subjected throughout his life as well as after it. He was only too aware of this block on a proper appreciation of his work, and wrote emphatically to his publisher, John Murray, to justify Cantos I and II of *Don Juan* after an uncertain reaction by the British public: 'You have been careless of this poem because some of your Synod don't approve of it – but I tell you – it will be long before you see anything half so good . . . I have read over the poem carefully – and I tell you *it is poetry*.'[12] This is the same 'carelessness' exhibited by Saintsbury. Because he disapproved of both the style and content of *Don Juan*, he dismissed it in a matter of paragraphs rather than stop and actually look at the verse itself, and in this respect, he was failing in his duty as a critic. The general feeling in his short comment on Byron is that here was something he knew was, in a sense, genuinely 'beyond' him, and the brevity of his remarks is the manifestation of that awareness. He completes his discussion with this candid admission:

> I have read Byron again and again; I have sometimes, by reading Byron only and putting a strong constraint upon myself, got nearly into the mood to enjoy him. But let eye or ear once catch sight or sound of real poetry, and the enchantment vanishes.[13]

As Bernard Beatty observes in his book *Byron's Don Juan*, ' "Thinking men" on the whole have not made conspicuously good readers of Byron's poetry.'[14]

However, one 'thinking man' who managed to read and appreciate Byron without 'putting a strong constraint' on himself, was Saintsbury's successor as Professor of English

Literature at Edinburgh, H. J. C. Grierson. His Warton Lecture on English Poetry, delivered on 24 November 1920, helped to haul Byron criticism out of the trough of Victorianism where it had languished for so long.

Grierson's lecture, which was published in the *Proceedings of the British Academy*, is a model of common sense and historical context. He confesses a slight bewilderment at the way his predecessor 'pursued Byron's reputation with a curious rancour which has not coloured his often equally severe criticism of Wordsworth and his heresies,' but then goes on to show that if Byron is put in a tradition, *not* of the 'greatest poetry' as Saintsbury would have it, but of Donne, Swift and especially Burns, then we can come to a much fairer assessment of his work.

Even on the well-trodden ground of the Scott/Byron comparison, Grierson sees that Byron's value has been misunderstood for too long. In Scott, scenery and setting are everything, but for Byron:

> His central theme is the infinite worth of love and courage and endurance . . . Byron did in those poems, as Tennyson said, 'give the world another heart and new pulses, and so we are kept going' . . . he delineated, as Wordsworth and none of his contemporaries did, passion and energy.[15]

It is this 'passion and energy' that brings him into line with that alternative tradition in poetry, the tradition of Donne, Rochester, Swift and Burns: poets who appear to be almost physically present in their best work. As Grierson says:

> Byron was a lover, masculine and passionate, as Donne and Burns had been before him . . . Just as Burns was a great poet who was also a peasant, a peasant who really lived the life and shared the joys of peasants . . . so Byron was a poet who was also a man among men, and a man of the world, seeing the world with which he was at war, through the eyes of the world.[16]

By virtue of his Scottish upbringing, Byron always had a great affection for the poetry of Burns, but his most ecstatic comments on the man were reserved for his letters, particularly the 'unpublished and never-to-be-published' ones. As he wrote in his *Journal* on 13 December 1813: 'They are full of oaths and obscene songs. What an antithetical mind! –

tenderness, roughness – delicacy, coarseness – sentiment, sensuality – soaring and grovelling, dirt and deity – all mixed up in that one compound of inspired clay!' It is significant that what appealed most to Byron was the curious eclecticism in Burns which so many readers, both then and now, have found in his own poetry and personality.

Grierson is less explicit about the nature of a comparison with Swift, and concentrates on their shared political interests and involvements rather than stressing any obvious point of poetical similarity. So, in the final paragraph of his lecture, Grierson says:

> But pure humour and sincere generous passion are (*Don Juan's*) finest qualities, the humour, the love of banter, the passionate hatred of cruelty and injustice which were as characteristic of the real Byron as of the real Swift, with whom he had so much in common.[17]

This is to emphasise their common humanity, but there is also a poetic point to be made between the two. Byron's best tales – most notably *Mazeppa* – are written in the octosyllabic couplets that Swift used almost exclusively, which bowl along with such an impression of speed and informality that it is a short step from there to the *ottava rima* stanzas of *Beppo* and *Don Juan*. This is almost contrary to Byron's stand on the heroic couplet, which he championed in his early output and continued to defend throughout his life, in the works of such second-rate poets as Campbell and Rogers, although it had very obviously had its day. Whilst it is true that some of Scott's verse tales are also written in the octosyllabic couplet, and therefore must be considered as a possible influence on Byron, there is a significant anecdote in Leslie Marchand's biography which adds weight to the Swift side of the balance. One of Byron's shipmates on his last voyage to Greece, James Hamilton Browne, recorded in voyeuristic detail the movements and activities of the poet, and at one point observed that he was reading Swift and 'thus supposed he was proposing to write another canto of *Don Juan*.'[18] Surely, as Grierson came close to saying, it was the rapid, incisive and colloquial couplets of Swift, rather than the decorative, evenly stressed narratives of Scott, that influenced the later works of Byron.

Grierson had edited Donne's poems in 1912, and it was that edition which helped re-establish not just Donne himself, but the whole 'Metaphysical' period into the accepted area of study and commentary. With our hindsight, the comparison between Donne and Byron seems obvious, but Grierson's penetrating analysis in 1920 was something quite new. Of Donne, he says: '(the) songs and sonnets have reasserted their worth after a long interval, because passion made Donne a subtle and at times even a profound thinker, and because his style, if harsh and careless, is never banal, and often splendidly felicitous.'[19] All these comments on Donne's style, especially, as we have seen, the one concerning his carelessness, have been made at some time or another about Byron – although usually with a less complimentary intent.

Later, talking about the Haidée and Juan interlude in Canto II of *Don Juan*, he claims: 'There is nothing like it in English poetry except some of the songs of Burns and the complex, vibrant passion, sensual and spiritual, of Donne's songs and elegies.'[20] Again, it is that 'complex, vibrant passion', which is the driving force behind an established but often unrecognised tradition in English and Scottish poetry, that Grierson is right to identify in Byron. He, more than anyone else before or since, combined genuine talent with personal charisma to create his own potent and enormously appealing poetic tone.

Byron was a true internationalist: born in England, raised in Scotland, finding his cultural home in Italy and his destiny in Greece – there is no one country that can claim a greater right to him than any other. Nevertheless, there has always been a Scottish view of him and his work: from Brougham and Jeffrey in *The Edinburgh Review* itself, through the impatience and disapproval of Saintsbury, and the wisdom and perspective of Grierson, right up to the clarity of W. W. Robson, whose 1957 article 'Byron as Improviser'[21] is still rightly considered to be one of the most influential in the field. Edinburgh is, in some sense, Byron's capital city – he was proud of his Scottish upbringing and spoke with a marked accent until the day he died – but in this most conservative of northern capitals, it is the advantage of *not* having the hot-blooded passion of the Mediterranean nations, nor the *laissez faire* of Regency London, that has enabled Edinburgh to keep Byron in clear focus. There has always been, and will always be, an Edinburgh view of Byron.

NOTES

1. Shelley to Byron, 20 November, 1816. The review which had prompted this remark was of Coleridge's 'Christabel'.
2. *The Edinburgh Review*, number XI (January, 1808), 285–9.
3. It has been pointed out that whenever Byron felt strongly about a subject in his letters, he invariably quoted from Shakespeare. The quotation here comes from *Much Ado About Nothing* II iii, and suggests that despite his dismissive tone, Byron is feeling the bad review quite keenly.
4. Byron to John Murray, 30 July 1821.
5. *Journal*, 22 November 1813.
6. Preface to the second edition, *English Bards and Scotch Reviewers*, 1809.
7. From 438–539.
8. *The Edinburgh Review*, number XXIX (February, 1818), 302–10.
9. *A History of Nineteenth Century Literature* (1896), 79.
10. Ibid., 80.
11. Ibid.
12. Byron to John Murray, 31 August 1821.
13. *A History of Nineteenth Century Literature*, 81.
14. *Byron's Don Juan* (1985), 222.
15. *Proceedings of the British Academy*, IX. The Warton Lecture on English Poetry, number XI, 'Lord Byron: Arnold and Swinburne', 10.
16. Ibid., 11–12.
17. Ibid., 31.
18. In Leslie A. Marchand, *Byron: A Biography* (1958), III, 1095.
19. Grierson, 10.
20. Ibid., 23.
21. W. W. Robson, 'Byron as Improviser' in *Proceedings of The British Academy*, 1957

Byron, Scott, and Nostalgia

J. DRUMMOND BONE

The cliché is that in every Conradian bar in the Far East some Scotsman drips tears into his drink, bewailing the good old Broomielaw – or that in quiet tea-parties in the Cotswolds soft accents sigh for the Moray Firth. And of course it goes without saying that *that* Broomielaw and *that* Moray Firth are nowhere to be found, and *were* nowhere to be found. Nostalgia is a matter not only of a place and a time, but of the passing of time in general, and of a feeling of dislocation in general. It localises that feeling of every day being cast from the garden, of existential loss. Or indeed it particularises the sense of loss as the sense of existence itself, for it could be said of our caricature Scots that their only true loss would be the loss of loss, for their identity is bound up with this emotion. But then of how many other peoples could this, in different ways, be said? Nostalgia is certainly a feeling which is positively indulged; though a feeling of loss, it is also a recovery of the past, and an odd affirmation of continuity in which we do not exist in isolated 'presents', but in the stream of time. I shall look at an extract from Scott and a few from Byron, examining their treatment of time and place lost, and noticing a gradual shift from nostalgia presented as the artistic recuperation of some quite definite 'real' loss – in which the recovery becomes a positively pleasant or even useful emotion – to nostalgia presented as the loss, not of something definite, but of the loss of the ability to *prevent the emotion of loss*, a nostalgia which does not have the perhaps sentimental ease of loss turned into positive feeling, but an absence indeed.

The following is taken from the Introduction to Canto II of *Marmion*, and was written in 1808. It takes the form of a verse letter from the author to the Rev. John Marriott, but it is a very stylised author.

119

The scenes are desert now, and bare,
Where flourish'd once a forest fair,
When these waste glens with copse were lin'd,
And peopled with the hart and hind.
Yon Thorn – perchance whose prickly spears
Have fenc'd him for three hundred years,
While fell around his green compeers –
Yon lonely Thorn, would he could tell
The changes of his parent dell,
Since he, so grey and stubborn now,
Wav'd in each breeze a sapling bough;
Would he could tell how deep the shade
A thousand mingled branches made;
How broad the shadows of the oak,
How clung the rowan to the rock,
And through the foliage show'd his head,
With narrow leaves and berries red;
What pines on every mountain sprung,
O'er every dell what birches hung,
In every breeze what aspens shook,
What alders shaded every brook!

'Here, in my shade,' methinks he'd say,
'The mighty stag at noontide lay:
The wolf I've seen, a fiercer game,
(The neighbouring dingle bears his name,)
With lurching step around me prowl,
And stop, against the moon to howl;
The mountain-boar, on battle set,
His tusks upon my stem would whet;
While doe, and roe, and red-deer good,
Have bounded by, . . .

From Yair – which hills so closely bind,
Scarce can the Tweed his passage find,
Though much he fret and chafe and toil
Till all his eddying currents boil, –
Her long-descended lord has gone,
And left us by the stream alone.

And much I miss those sportive boys,
Companions of my mountain joys,
Just at the age 'twixt boy and youth,
When thought is speech, and speech is truth.
Close to my side, with what delight
They press'd to hear of Wallace wight,
When pointing to his airy mound,
I call'd his ramparts holy ground! . . .

When, musing on companions gone,
We doubly feel ourselves alone,
Something, my friend, we yet may gain;
There is a pleasure in this pain:
It soothes the love of lonely rest,
Deep in each gentler heart impress'd.
'Tis silent amid worldly toils,
And stifled soon by mental broils;
But, in a bosom thus prepar'd,
Its still small voice is often heard,
Whispering a mingled sentiment,
'Twixt resignation and content.[1]

The past before this forest clearance is clearly intended as a
historical one. If the thorn could speak, that past would be
recoverable. But it is also linked with images of holiness
(Wallace's 'holy' ramparts) – and of innocent community (his
young companions 'close to his side'), and the land has the
plenty of a Paradise (in the listing of the trees and game).

Scott had clearly been reading his Wordsworth fairly closely
– the 'sportive boys' may have something to do with the 'little
lines of sportive wood' in 'Tintern Abbey', and there are other
verbal echoes of the 'Intimations' Ode too, as well as the
generally similar tone.[2] Quite explicitly, the sense of Paradise
lost is seen not as a wholly unpleasant sensation, on the
contrary, it informs the spiritual emptiness of the present
('There is a pleasure in this pain/It soothes the love of lonely
rest'). The lost past is fuller than the alive now, and clearly
with the reader's interest in that past, the sense of loss is filled
by the plenitude of memory. Our own feelings as readers are

identified with the loss made positive, and we feel – arguably sentimentally – reassured.

Now this is a relatively easy process for literature, since it exists inevitably as a positive and not a negative quantity. As good Derrideans we know that if you seek presence in language you will find only absence – the odd corollary of which is that the absence of absence is presence, of a sort.[3] It is difficult to be negative, for the negative not to be turned into a positive just by virtue of its expression. A sense of meaning-lessness becomes a meaningful sense of meaninglessness if we read about it. Let us note again the line 'When thought is speech, and speech is truth'. Here is a picture of an ideal language, a guaranteed chain from truth to thought to speech, where speech *is* presencing. This for Scott's speaker is clearly a possibility, though now lost to him along with his idyllic childhood. There is scarcely even a hint that though it was possible, it is now and for ever impossible; for us, as for the narrator, this more general reading is suppressed in the (oddly) more hopeful 'such feelings pure,/They will not, cannot, long endure' (not quoted above).[4] The statement of loss here carries with it the emotion of its potential recovery. This sense of intermingled loss and the recovery of either presence in language or paradise in life – the two are, if not identical, very nearly so – is the stuff of nostalgia, at least if we accept that nostalgia is intrinsically un-self-critical. But the frequent admixture of irony – even in the case of the maudlin exile on his bar-stool – might suggest that this is not a total account of the nostalgic dynamic.

Byron takes up the same identification as Scott of the loss of the past with the loss of the ability of language to live. In the fragment 'Harmodia' we find:

'The things that were' – and what and whence were they,
Those clouds and rainbows of thy yesterday? . . .
Such is the past – the light of other days
That shines but warms not with its powerless rays
A moonbeam someone watches to behold
Distinct but distant – clear – but deathlike cold.
Oh, as full thought comes rushing o'er the mind,

Of all we saw before – to leave behind –
Of all – but words – what are they? can they give
A trace of breath to thoughts while yet they live?
No – Passion, Feeling speak not – or in vain –
The tear for Grief, the groan must speak for Pain . . .
The strife once o'er, then words may find their way,
Yet how enfeebled from the forced delay.[5]

Memory is not a means to recovery of the past here – on the
contrary, memory reinforces the sense of alienation from the
past ('Distinct, but distant'). Words reinforce the absence of
the feelings of which they speak, and only inarticulate noise
seems to carry the life of a thought. Thoughts are dead by the
time they are expressed in language, as the past is realised as
past in memory. This is not a matter of an incident of nostalgia,
but of loss as the condition of life in time. There is no previous
life of perfect communication which has been lost, no sense of
a full but lost past, only the sense of passing. What memory
laments here is memory itself. It is rather the inevitable
inscription of loss than the preservation or recovery of some
specific past and place. This is an early example of Byron's
bleaker use of nostalgic emotion – bleaker that is than Scott's –
but it is arguably simply a different thing from essential
nostalgia – an interpretation of memory which denies the
pleasantness which is perhaps central to the nostalgic
moment. If certain uses of nostalgia uncritically recuperate the
past in the guise of mourning its loss, so perhaps Byron's use
of memory here is equally monovocal in its nihilism. It is not
really a *critical* nostalgia.

'Harmodia' evolved into one of the best known of the *Hebrew
Melodies*, 'Sun of the Sleepless'. The genre in which Byron
found himself writing without question both produced and
constrained the characteristic tone of the poems of exile and
nostalgia in *Hebrew Melodies*. To a large extent his model is
Moore, and this of course gives us a Celtic connection. Clearly
the Jewish diaspora was a subject to which Byron was already
susceptible.[6] But this heroic context enforced techniques to
which one might say he was all too readily susceptible, having
exercised them to the point of mannerism in *Childe Harold* I-II

and the already written members of the Turkish Tale sequence.[7] These all tend to produce a version of the past lost as absolute recovery. 'On Jordan's Banks' is a case in point:

> On Jordan's banks the Arab's camels stray,
> On Sion's hill the False One's votaries pray,
> The Baal-adorer bows on Sinai's steep –
> Yet there – even there – Oh God! thy thunders sleep:
>
> There – where thy finger scorch'd the tablet stone!
> There – where thy shadow to thy people shone!
> Thy glory shrouded in its garb of fire:
> Thyself – none living see and not expire!
>
> Oh! in the lightning let thy glance appear!
> Sweep from his shiver'd hand the oppressor's spear:
> How long by tyrants shall thy land be trod?
> How long thy temple worshipless, Oh God?[8]

The essence of the technique is to freeze time and concentrate space into a point. We note the repetitive 'There' – exactly 'there', and the climactic rise from 'thy glory' to the absolute revelation 'thyself', and the repeated negatives defining this moment – 'none living', 'not expire'. The aporia captures the moment of the lightning, out of grammatical time, and the insistent questions do not elicit a temporal answer, but on the contrary invoke an immediate presence at the climax and the end of the poem, on the dramatic direct appeal to the presence of God. For the purpose of future comparison we note too the firm consonant rhyme, with its closed ending and precise moment of enunciation – trod, God. Here, now. The ecstasy of loss has become an act of recovery. It might again be true that such ecstasy is only tangentially nostalgic however. More obviously to our point is the 'By the Rivers of Babylon'[9] in which the withholding of the song becomes the preservation of the past as still alive. That is, the loss of the place in which to sing the song becomes through the act of denial (through an affirmation of loss, in other words), a recovery of the meaning of itself. Again the rhetoric is full of evers and nevers, and precise moments. Still one does not want to say that even most

of the *Hebrew Melodies* works the same way. The last stanza of
'The Wild Gazelle', and curiously enough that fine variation
on a sonnet which begins with the definitive phrase 'It is the
hour'[10] are more genuinely negative, for example, and 'Sun of
the Sleepless' itself is one of Byron's finest evocations of loss,
using many of the techniques we shall look at below, and
which are perhaps more characteristic of the late poems.

Byron's experience of exile became real enough, of course.
His was not only a displacement in time, a sense of constantly
lost youth – Byron felt old from childhood as the merest glance
at his letters will show[11] – but an exile in physical fact. In
stanzas 8-10 of *Childe Harold* IV, relatively new to the exile's
state, he contemplates his relationship with Britain:

> I've taught me other tongues – and in strange eyes
> Have made me not a stranger; to the mind
> Which is itself, no changes bring surprise;
> Nor is it harsh to make, nor hard to find
> A country with – ay, or without mankind;
> Yet was I born where men are proud to be,
> Not without cause; and should I leave behind
> The inviolate island of the sage and free,
> And seek me out a home by a remoter sea,
>
>   Perhaps I loved it well: and should I lay
> My ashes in a soil which is not mine,
> My spirit shall resume it – if we may
> Unbodied choose a sanctuary. I twine
> My hopes of being remembered in my line
> With my land's language: if too fond and far
> These aspirations in their scope incline, –
> If my fame should be, as my fortunes are,
> Of hasty growth and blight, and dull Oblivion bar
>
> My name from out the temple where the dead
> Are honoured by the nations – let it be –
> And light the laurels on a loftier head!
> And be the Spartan's epitaph on me –
> 'Sparta hath many a worthier son than he.'

Meantime I seek no sympathies, nor need;
The thorns which I have reaped are of the tree
I planted, – they have torn me, – and I bleed:
I should have known what fruit would spring from such
    a seed.[12]

The 'quotation' from Milton, which he also used at the end of
Manfred, somewhat undercuts the possibilities of belonging
implied in 'not a stranger', already rather tenuously dependent on the still '*strange* eyes' (my emphasis), and this sense of
isolation is increased in the qualification 'or without mankind'.
The lost land can be reached in death, and through the poet's
art becoming part of its tradition. The rhetoric which suggests
the contrary – that he might be forgotten, condemned to an
exile from not only his land but the tradition of his language for
eternity – is duplicitous, for it makes heroic the imagined
absence of heroic status. We note the grandiose repetition of
the phrases 'And . . .', the quotation from the classical epitaph
(precisely from the heroic age), and the really rather blasphe-
mous possibilities in the image of the thorns, together with the
blustering emphasis (particularly in the penultimate line) on
the first person, with its emphatic assumption of responsibility
for its own fate. The nostalgia here is still productive of an
emotion which, at least in its force and assertion, can be
characterised as positive. Its effect on the reader is to render
isolation and loss as heroism and plenitude, all the more so
since the imagined loss is two-fold – a real one in the past, and
a possible further one in the future. Both, however, are
accommodated into the grandeur of their present assumption.
The pause at the end of the first stanza quoted, and the
enjambement of the next, are ringingly resolved by the full
close of the last, with the 'I''s dramatic assertion of its
understanding, the climax of a movement which has really
run through the three stanzas. But just as the *Hebrew
Melodies* partly conditioned the presentation of nostalgia and
exile by virtue of its 'national poem' genre, so here one
suspects that Childe Harold the character is imposing on his
author.

Even by 1816 – in the 'Epistle to Augusta' for example –

another tone is beginning to dominate.[13] We however shall pursue it in a later form, in an example from *Don Juan*:

> No more – no more – Oh! never more on me
>   The freshness of the heart can fall like dew,
> Which out of all the lovely things we see
>   Extracts emotions beautiful and new,
> Hived in our bosoms like the bag o' the bee:
>   Think'st thou the honey with those objects grew?
> Alas! 'twas not in them, but in thy power
> To double even the sweetness of a flower.[14]

The stanza begins with the characteristic absolute negation, but the repetition, with the rhetorical pause of the dash and the 'Oh!' which 'lapses' again from inarticulacy into words, spreads it into time – the negative becomes an ongoing state in this repetition, and this impression of time passing is helped by the comparative suggestion of 'more'. The climax of this negative journey is reached by way of the 'Oh', which might take us back to the sighs of 'Harmodia', or on to the syncopes and singulti of *Don Juan* XV, 'emblems of emotion' stacked against the great Ennui.[15] Here is the real loss, indicatable, but not expressible. But this inexpressible is not uncritically allowed to remain hanging outside of time, for the rest of the stanza becomes almost a gloss upon it. The two syllables of 'never' – as much as its more specific negative – make it stand as the climax of the articulate line, though it is the vowel assonance of the 'o' which has completely dominated the line until this point which really paces the rise of the line to the inarticulate climax of 'oh'. This climax is in fact dissolved by the change of vowel sound on 'never'. The next three lines take us into the world of nostalgia, and the tense is notably present in effect – can, see, extracts. The enjambement keeps the reader moving on apace in the search for the delayed verb, and it is partly the release of this control of breath, as it were, which produces the remarkable modulation on 'fall', a release with an ambiguous overtone played up by the two-edged possibility in its alliterative connection with 'freshness' – whether that is a link or a contrast – and a release saved from a trite stasis by the fact that one cannot savour it at the end of a line. Line three highlights the simplicity of 'lovely' emerging from the context of the monosyllabic grammatical particles which precede it, and inviting us to be aware of its full force – things which invite love. Interestingly, too, Byron is royally unconcerned that what he says in lines 3-4 does not make clear sense, given what he is about to say. Here the heart extracts emotions 'out of all the lovely things we see', but in the very next line we learn that these emotions are 'hived in our bosoms like the bag o' the bee', and for a moment it is quite unclear whether they are, as the metaphor demands, stored after extraction, or whether as the grammar really suggests, they are somehow 'hived' at the moment of extraction. The past participle, hanging at a transition of tense, contributes to the awkwardness. The doubt of course is at the heart of the stanza – in youth we believe the emotions to spring out of the 'lovely things', but in age, the stanza tells us later, we learn that we have created them ourselves. This shift is packed into lines 3-4-5, and line 6 then draws the problem to the reader's attention – did you notice? did that surprise you? – 'Think'st thou the honey with those objects grew?' The tense at the end of the line slips now firmly back into the past, and we are returned to the world of loss, the negative. All the rhymes of this stanza, relatively close in relationship to play down the possible energy gained from emphasis at the line-ending, have been open, allowing the voice to diminuendo at its own speed, and that remains true even of the consonantal ending of the couplet, whether we pronounce it in Scots or English. But here the diminuendo effect is more strongly and unambiguously marked by the double rhyme or elision (I do not want to get involved in the argument about which it should be – the last line is almost impossible to decide on, because of the other possibility for elision in 'even') – the point is that the lines have an irresistible removal of emphasis at their end, and scarcely really 'end'. Here too the possible inversion of the effect of the answer 'No' is avoided in the introductory avoidance of a direct answer – alas. What is gone too has no universal pretension to it – it is 'only' the sweetness of a flower (the indefinite article here too is so right). In its very modesty, of course, lies the real sorrow.

Here what is lost is not, though it appears to be, a real Eden –

it is the ability to turn the world we know into an Eden which has gone. Loss as the human condition is, then, an experience of loss of real or hypothetical energy of the heart, spiritual energy, imagination – not the loss of a real or hypothetical country, or time, or object of love. Here loss is genuinely a state of mind, an inability to love. But even more importantly, this loss is carefully never allowed to monumentalise itself into the presence of loss, so to speak, it does not turn the experience of absence into the experience of presence, a lived experience of sadness into a literary experience of sentimental fullness. We are not allowed to dwell on the experience of loss for so long that it becomes an absolute and flips into a positive.

Of course in the next stanza Byron actually more or less makes this point explicit:

No more – no more – Oh! never more, my heart,
    Can thou be my sole world, my universe!
Once all in all, but now a thing apart,
    Thou canst not be my blessing or my curse:
The illusion's gone for ever, and thou art
    Insensible, I trust, but none the worse,
And in thy stead I've got a deal of judgment,
Though heaven knows how it ever found a lodgement.[16]

He returns to the vocabulary of single absolutes to describe how his emotions once seemed to him. But that absolute world of 'sole worlds', 'universes', 'all in alls', is now gone – not 'filled' however by absolute emptiness, not replaced by a chiasmic reversal of itself. No, the gap is somewhat covered by 'a deal of judgment' in exchange – and note too that half-way quantity, 'a deal'. Nor of course is it filled by the memory of a once complete, though now vanished, past, for the memory of completeness is qualified by the fact of memory. Taking the two stanzas together there is, however, a feeling for the joys of the past, but a feeling too that they are inevitably past. These two intertwine to give the sense that the nostalgic experience itself, if self-aware, affirms the true passage of time at the same time as it attempts to overcome it. And in tragic, ironic, sweetness it locates the passage of time in our human inability to possess our own experience.

NOTES

1. J. Logie Robertson, ed., *The Poetical Works of Sir Walter Scott*, Oxford, 1894, 100–2.
2. *Tintern Abbey*, ll. 15–16. The general sense of the transition from boyhood to youth is also paralleled in ll. 65–83.
3. 'History and knowledge . . . have always been determined . . . as detours *for the purpose* of the reappropriation of presence.' Or: 'All signifiers . . . are derivative with regard to what would wed the voice indissolubly to the mind or to the thought of the signified sense, indeed to the thing itself . . .'. Jacques Derrida, *Of Grammatology*, trans. G. C. Spivak, The Johns Hopkins University Press, 1976, 10 and 11. 'Absence' is as un-presence-able as any 'thing' else.
4. Scott, op. cit., 102.
5. All Byron quotations are from J. J. McGann, ed., *Lord Byron: The Complete Poetical Works*, Clarendon Press, Oxford. Hereafter McGann. Here vol. III, 1981, 275.
6. For discussion of the circumstances surrounding the composition of *Hebrew Melodies* see F. Burwick and P. Douglass, eds., *Byron and Nathan: A Selection of Hebrew Melodies*, North Carolina University Press, 1988; and of the national genre in particular, Thomas L. Ashton, ed., *Byron's Hebrew Melodies*, Routledge and Kegan Paul, 1972, 3–61.
7. *The Giaour, The Bride of Abydos, The Corsair,* and *Lara*. I have discussed these techniques in 'The Rhetoric of Freedom', in Alan Bold, ed., *Byron: Wrath and Rhyme*, Barnes and Noble and Vision, 1983, 166–85.
8. McGann, III. 293.
9. McGann, III. 308–9.
10. McGann, III. 297–8. The poem begins with a quatrain but proceeds in couplets. It is of 14 lines. The space of the quatrain rhymes is collapsed into the 'simultaneity' of the couplets, and the residual sonnet possibility is dissolved in this structural looseness — 'As twilight melts beneath the moon away' (l. 14).
11. For example Leslie Marchand's *Byron's Letters and Journals*, Murray, 1973–1982, letter of October 15, 1816, to Augusta, V, 119–20.
12. McGann, vol. II, p. 127.
13. McGann, vol. IV, 1986, pp. 35–40. Stanzas 8–11 are particularly to the point, in which Byron swings between the beauty of Lake Leman before him, and the memory of Augusta and the lake at Newstead in his memory. The

attempt to accommodate the memory to the present, and its
failure, reaches towards an emptier nostalgia than the more
public *Childe Harold* III.
14. McGann, vol. V, 1986, 77. This stanza and the one
following it (i.e. 214 and 215) were added by Byron at proof
stage. They were not however written *before* the subsequent
stanzas, as is sometimes alleged, and were among the last
stanzas added to the first Canto. Indeed the reprise of the
train of thought from 213 is clear at 216. 214 and 215
essentially expand the thought of stanzas which though
not in Byron's first draft predated them. See McGann, V.
665.
15. McGann, V. 589.

> Ah! – What should follow slips from my reflection:
>   Whatever follows ne'ertheless may be
> As àpropos of hope or retrospection,
>   As though the lurking thought had follow'd free.
> All present life is but an Interjection,
>   An 'Oh!' or 'Ah!' of joy or misery,
> Or a 'Ha! ha!' or 'Bah!' – a yawn, or 'Pooh!'
> Of which perhaps the latter is most true.
>
> But, more or less, the whole's a syncopé,
>   Or a singultus — emblems of Emotion,
> The grand Antithesis to great Ennui,
>   Wherewith we break our bubbles on the ocean,
> That Watery Outline of Eternity,
>   Or miniature at least, as is my notion,
> Which ministers unto the soul's delight,
> In seeing matters which are out of sight.

16. McGann, V. 77–8. Andrew Cooper puts Byron's refusal to
polarise hope and despair nicely: 'Byron's skepticism is less
a definite philosophic rationalism than a perpetual process
of pragmatic adjustment.' *Doubt and Identity in Romantic
Poetry*, Yale University Press, 1988, p. 145.

'The Island': Scotland, Greece and Romantic Savagery

ANGUS CALDER

The Island is Byron's last narrative poem, a tale set in the South Seas. It contains a passage very commonly cited as proof that Byron was still, or increasingly, attached to Scotland. It refers to the love between a Polynesian woman and a Scottish sailor:

> Both children of the isles, though distant far;
> Both born beneath a sea-presiding star;
> Both nourish'd amidst nature's native scenes,
> Loved to the last, whatever intervenes
> Between us and our childhood's sympathy,
> Which still reverts to what first caught the eye.
> He who first met the Highlands' swelling blue
> Will love each peak that shows a kindred hue,
> Hail in each crag a friend's familiar face,
> And clasp the mountain in his mind's embrace.
> Long have I roamed through lands which are not mine,
> Adored the Alp, and loved the Appennine,
> Revered Parnassus, and beheld the steep
> Jove's Ida and Olympus crown the deep;
> But 'twas not all long ages' love, nor all
> *Their* nature held me in their thrilling thrall;
> The infant rapture still survived the boy,
> And Loch-na-gar with Ida look'd o'er Troy,
> Mix'd Celtic memories with the Phrygian mount,
> And Highland linns with Castalie's clear fount.
> (Canto The Second, XII)

What is the real significance of this passage?

In April 1823 Byron wrote to the young Count D'Orsay, whose acquaintance he had just made, as a weary middle-aged man of the world:

132

. . . Though I love my country, I do not love my country-
men – at least, such as they now are . . . Live while you
can; and that you may have the full enjoyment of the many
advantages of youth, talent, and figure, which you possess,
is the wish of an – Englishman, – I suppose, but it is
no treason; for my mother was Scotch, and my name and
family are both Norman; and as for myself, I am of no
country.[1]

Byron was in what proved to be his last phase of intensive
creativity. He had not long finished a satire in couplets, *The
Age of Bronze* and was working still on the English cantos of
Don Juan. He had found time to compose *The Island* during five
weeks from mid-January to mid-February. Such variety of
subject matter and styles, and the pace at which he wrote
at this time, demonstrated his chameleon-like capacity. He
had not one literary personality, but several, and he developed them with reckless fluency. *The Island*, in parts, was as
sweetly lyrical as *Juan* was worldly-wise and acidulous.
Composing faces to meet the faces that he met, he presented
a very different Byron to D'Orsay from the one who had
written to Walter Scott just over a year before, exclaiming
that he carried the Waverley novels everywhere although
he already had them by heart, and who had insisted in the
Tenth Canto of *Juan* that he was 'half a Scot and bred a whole
one.'

It is not in Byron's letters, or in the few scattered references
to Scotland in his vast poetic output, that we can find evidence
to convince us that Byron was a Scottish poet, or, indeed, to
prove the contrary. He *said*, to D'Orsay at least, that he was not
a *traitor* to England when he attacked its prevailing values
because he was not *really* English anyway, but whether he *felt*
as identified with Scotland as he intimated to Scott is not
possible to estimate. This does not mean, though, that we
cannot follow T.S. Eliot, Leavis and other distinguished
literary scholars in arguing that the character of his verse is
largely, or wholly, explicable only in terms of his half-admitted
Scottishness.

There are three overlapping bases for such an argument.
One is provided by undisputed biographical facts. He was

brought up until the age of ten in Aberdeen by a mother proud of ancient Scottish lineage, who spoke with a strong Buchan accent. He was seduced by a Scottish serving girl when aged, probably, only nine. He attended schools in Aberdeen. In view of all this, his admiration for Burns and devotion to Scott involve more than his subscribing to current literary fashion: they would speak to and reach such a reader as they could not touch a purely English writer. Hence – our second basis – the arguments which account for features of his styles (I use the plural) by relating them to Scottish tradition are inherently plausible. I think that Tom Scott was unwise to accept T.S. Eliot's rather silly case that Byron writes English like an 'intelligent foreigner', and I am not sure that Eliot's more seductive notion that Byron's attacks on Southey are in the 'flyting' tradition of Dunbar and Montgomerie can be sustained as Tom Scott assumes – where is the evidence that Byron read Middle Scots verse? But Tom Scott's own point that Byron learnt how to use the Spenserian stanza not from *The Faerie Queene*, but from Thomson and Beattie, both eighteenth-century Scots writing in English, is firm enough, and his own experiments in transcribing passages from Byron into Scots are delightfully convincing.[2] The comparison of Byron with Burns was first made by Walter Scott; and when Byron wrote in enthusiasm about Burns's letters in his journal in 1813, he used terms which others have applied to him: 'What an antithetical mind! – tenderness, roughness, delicacy, coarseness – sentiment, sensuality – soaring and grovelling, dirt and deity – all mixed up in that one compound of inspired clay.'[3] Roderick S. Speer, who quotes this, has argued for Byron's Scottishness on a third basis, an ideological one. Irrespective of his subject matter, which is only very rarely Scottish, Byron displays throughout his work traits familiar in Scottish tradition. He believes in human fatedness. (We might call this belief Byron's 'secular Calvinism'.) The pressure exerted by this fatalism finds outlet in 'self assertive exuberance and extravagance'. (If we are doomed, we may as we have fun when we can: and why take life seriously at all?) Finally, Byron has an ambivalent appreciation of the 'antithetical' nature of human kind – 'soaring and grovelling, dirt and deity' – as Lyndsay and Burns had had, as MacDiarmid and Grassic Gibbon would have after him.[4]

If this line of argument is right – and I think it is very plausible – Byron's specific references to Scotland in his last verse tale *The Island* are no more and no less 'Scottish' than his handling of 'The Prisoner of Chillon' or of English manners in *Don Juan*. His Scottishnness is assumed to be involuntary, the product of his earliest social conditioning in which balladry and the Bible intermingled. My own thrust here is to show that the high romantic sentiment attached to these Scottish references is interesting less because of its autobiographical slanting than because it shows Byron, like Scott before him, developing the discourse of poetic tartanry – but, being Byron, he gives this discourse an individual and rather extreme application.

The Island has not enjoyed much critical attention, still less esteem. Bernard Blackstone, who does consider it at some length, calls it 'the escapist poem *par excellence*.'[5] But Michael Cooke argues that the regression to infantile irresponsibility which Blackstone detected is in fact only on the poem's surface. The poet allows his young lovers to escape to an idyllic sanctuary from the sphere of civilised crime and retribution, but their absolution is 'not shared by Byron'.[6] The poem in fact presents two opposite versions of morality and does not attempt to reconcile them; like earlier verse tales by Byron (but unlike Scott's narrative poems), *The Island* creates moral suspense and refuses finally to resolve it. It offers a fictitious version of the fate of the *Bounty* mutineers, in which all perish at last, hunted down by British justice, except a young Scotsman who is rescued by a Polynesian Princess.

How seriously did Byron take this performance? He wrote *The Island* at a time when he was very serious indeed about producing more and more cantos of *Don Juan* in defiance of British reviewers, of the public's prudery, of his own friends' judgement, and that of his publisher John Murray. He had fallen out with Murray and meanwhile, with admirable self-sacrifice, shouldered as a kind of legacy from his beloved dead friend Shelley the burden of helping Leigh Hunt (who had come to Italy and was now dependent on him), and

Hunt's publisher brother John. He had contributed his great *Vision of Judgement* to the first number of *The Liberal*, a magazine edited by Leigh and brought out by John Hunt. At odds with Murray, he instructed his agent to give *The Island* to John, and also the last eleven finished cantos of *Don Juan*. One might infer from the circumstances that Byron reverted to the form of a short verse tale with a Byronic hero (Fletcher Christian) of his old type, mixing high romantic passages about love with exciting action and surprisingly firm patriotic, pro-British sentiment, in the hope that its sales might enable him to get the sponger Leigh Hunt, with his prudish wife and intolerable children, off his hands. He showed it to Leigh Hunt, who was critical, then coolly responded that he knew the poem was somewhat tame, but that he did not want to 'run counter to the reigning stupidity altogether – otherwise they will say that I am eulogising *Mutiny*.' It seems that he was courting sections of the public whose conventional moral views he despised. He presented a different, though equally cool face to his agent Kinnaird, sending the poem to him with the comment that it was too long for *The Liberal*, 'not good enough perhaps to publish alone,' but would 'make a respectable figure' in a future collection of his writings'.[7] (Nevertheless it was published alone a few months later.)

Byron had often belittled his own work, though, and it is easy to see what attracted him to the story of the *Bounty* Mutiny. He acknowledged two sources for his poem – Lieutenant William Bligh's own account of his voyage and the Mutiny (1790), and an interesting work on the Tonga Islands recently compiled by a London doctor named John Martin (1816), which would have given him copious information about Polynesian customs and language. A third element which he fused into the poem was his current obsession with the struggle of the Greek people for liberation. He left for Greece, abandoning even *Don Juan*, to serve that struggle in July 1823, just six months after writing *The Island*. The stanza which I quoted at the outset of this piece digresses, of course, from the South Seas to Greece. Let us see what he does with these three elements.

The case can quite easily be made that William Bligh, far

from being the brutal despot of Hollywood legend, was a humane commander by the standards of his time. His own account of his voyage to Tahiti to collect breadfruit plants for transmission to Jamaica, where plantation owners hoped to feed their slaves on the fruit, certainly exaggerates the good order prevailing before the sudden mutiny when the ship was homeward bound, on 28 April 1789. But Byron had every reason to hail him as a 'gallant chief' at the outset of his first Canto, which describes Bligh's abrupt arousal at dawn by the mutineers, and the grim scenes which preceded the division of the crew. Eighteen men, with Bligh, were forced into a small boat with scanty provisions; the courage and skill with which Bligh steered it 3900 miles to the Dutch East Indies are evoked in Byron's ninth stanza. His account follows Bligh's own closely. How could the creator of *The Corsair* have resisted the last exchange between Bligh and Fletcher Christian, the Mutiny's leader and (probably) sole instigator? Christian has 'seemed as if meditating destruction on himself and every one else.' Bligh upbraids him, reminding him of the kindnesses which he has shown him. To which Christian replies, ' "That, – Captain Bligh, – that is the thing; – I am in hell – I am in hell." '[8]

As for the twenty-five men left aboard, some were clearly reluctant to stay. Bligh is surprisingly generous when attributing motives to the mutineers proper: '. . . I can only conjecture, that the mutineers had flattered themselves with the hopes of a more happy life among the Otaheitans [Tahitians], than they could possibly enjoy in England.' The men had established 'female connections'; Polynesian women were 'handsome, mild and cheerful in their manners and conversation', and had 'sufficient delicacy to make them admired and beloved.' The local chiefs liked the sailors and pressed them to stay, even promising them 'large possessions'. Sailors who had no prospects of a better life on shipboard or at home in Britain 'imagined it in their power to fix themselves in the midst of plenty, on one of the finest islands in the world, where they need not labour.'[9] This seems excessively fair and essentially true. When he wrote his account, Bligh did not know the sequel.

Christian sailed the *Bounty* from the Tongan island off which he had mutinied back to Tahiti. On the way, his ship called at Tubuai, one of a group known now as the Austral Islands (a French dependency). The natives were hostile, but the mutineers decided to settle there. They recruited twenty-four Tahitians, returned, and attempted to build a fort. Here Christian himself now faced mutiny, due to the shortage of women in his party, and his men voted two to one to return to Tahiti. After murdering scores of native islanders in a nasty punitive expedition, the *Bounty* men duly sailed back to the scene of their earlier fond 'connections'. Only nine of the twenty-five then then proceeded with Christian and some Tahitians to Pitcairn Island, where they were safe from British justice, but soon fell to murdering each other, till only one adult male, a white, was left alive – just sufficient to preserve a tiny patriarchal community. [10]

This was accidentally discovered by an American ship in 1808, and a British ship called at Pitcairn in 1814. So Christian's destination and death were known to many in Britain when Byron wrote his poem. However, he seems to have missed this new information. He believed that Tubuai, which he misspelt Toobonai, had been the last known port of call for Christian, and made that the scene of his poem. Furthermore, he took the liberty of assuming that the last four mutineers, including Christian, had been hunted down by an avenging British naval vessel. Something like this had indeed occurred on Tahiti, where Captain Edward Edwards had arrived in the *Pandora* nearly two years after the Mutiny, some of the *Bounty* men there had at once given themselves up, but a few had fled and had been pursued. Eventually ten men were brought home alive to stand court martial, six were sentenced to death, of whom two were pardoned. No gory last stand by four reckless men such as Byron recounts in his poem ever occurred.

There had been several Scots among the mutineers. McIntosh had been forced to stay on the *Bounty*, had begged Bligh to remember that he had no hand in the conspiracy, and was eventually pardoned. McCoy went with Christian to Pitcairn, where, as a former employee in a whisky distillery, he continued to manufacture some creature and was either pushed, or fell drunkenly, off a cliff. But the Norse name of

Byron's young hero, Torquil, and a reference to the Pentland
Firth, suggest that Byron hazily supposed that Orkney was
mountainous – for an Orcadian midshipman, George Stewart,
was certainly Byron's model. He came from what Bligh called
a 'creditable' parentage in Orkney, where Bligh himself had
been warmly entertained by Stewart's people. He had a liaison
with a high-born Tahitian, who died, of a broken heart it was
said, after he had surrendered to Edwards. Their child was
eventually brought up by missionaries. Stewart himself had
perished in the shipwreck of Edwards' *Pandora* off Australia,
with three other mutineers. Though he had shared whole-
heartedly in the mutiny, and may even have put the idea into
Christian's head, it suited a fellow midshipman, when he was
eventually court martialled, to claim that the dead Stewart had
been innocent. By 1831, when Sir John Barrow compiled what
seemed to be a definitive account of the mutiny and its sequel,
Stewart's purity of soul was taken for granted.[11] But Byron,
very Byronically, makes Torquil defiant till almost the last,
when just as pursuers close in for the kill, he is spirited away
by Neuha, to a secret and very remarkable cave.

Such a cave as Byron describes existed, not off Tubuai, but in
the Tongan group. He learnt about it in John Martin's *Account
of the Natives of the Tonga Islands* (1816). Martin had never been
to the Pacific, but constructed a readable and convincing book
from what he was told by William Mariner who, as a young
sailor aged fourteen on a privateer sailing in 1805, was spared
when Tongan natives seized his ship and murdered most of
the crew, was 'adopted' by an island chief, and lived for four
years in the Polynesian fashion. His lord once went to the
small island of Hoonga to shoot birds and rats. Thus Mariner
came to enter a wonderful cave, invisible from sea or land
because its only entrance was always below the surface of the
ocean: a submarine passage eight or nine feet long led to a
space some forty feet high by forty feet wide, with shelves on
its sides where one could sit and lie. Here, as the hunting party
drank *Kava*, Mariner heard the tale of the cavern's discoverer, a
young chief diving for turtle, who kept its existence a secret.
His island had a tyrant chief. When a lord revolted against
him, all his family were condemned to death. The young

turtle-hunting chief loved one of the rebels' daughters and persuaded her to flee with him in a canoe to the secret cavern, where he sustained her with mats, dress and food until it was safe to carry her to Fiji.

Byron, despite transferring the cavern to another island group, sticks closely to Martin's working of Mariner's story which the learned doctor freely embellishes with European sentiment – 'How happy were they in this solitary retreat! Tyrannic power now longer reached them. Shut out from the world and all its cares and perplexities . . . themselves were the only powers they served . . . (etc.)' Byron adopts (Canto 4, Stanza 6) the comparison, which Martin attributes to Mariner, of the Cavern's interior to that of a Gothic cathedral.[12]

He also transferred to the Austral Islands some Tongan words from the lexicon provided by Martin in an appendix, and, in another act of 'poetical liberty', self-confessed in a footnote, one of the songs set down from Mariner's memory. Anyone wondering why Macpherson's 'Ossianic' writings had carried such conviction sixty years before will find a kind of explanation here. Contemporary conventions dominate 'translation' at any one time. 'Ossian' might well have looked similar had it been wholly genuine. Witness the process by which an orally transmitted song, given in Tongan and word-by-word translation in Martin's appendix, is mediated through Martin's age-of-sentiment prose into Byron's freely Romantic version, 'sung' by Neuha to Torquil in three stanzas at the start of his second canto. Byron claimed that he had 'altered and added but . . . retained as much as possible of the original'.

The would-be literal:

As our minds (are) reflecting the great wind whistles towards us from the great (lofty) Toa trees in the inland upon the plain.

Is (to) me (the) mind large, beholding the surf below, endeavouring in vain to tear away the rocks firm. . . .

becomes in Martin's version in the main text:

. . . The whistling of the wind among the branches of the lofty *toa* shall fill us with a pleasing melancholy: or our minds shall be seized with astonishment as we behold the

roar of the surf below, endeavouring but in vain to tear away
the firm rocks . . .
then Byron's:

> And we will sit in twilight's face, and see
> The sweet moon glancing through the tooa tree,
> The lofty accents of whose sighing bough
> Shall sadly please us as we lean below;
> Or climb the steep, and view the surf in vain
> Wrestle with rocky giants o'er the main.

Anyone who has heard Ravel's *Chansons madécasses* well sung
knows that in the rhetoric of Byron's period, serious pro-
'native', anti-colonial feeling may lie locked – Ravel in the
1920s set Evariste Parny's late eighteenth century 'Madagas-
can' prose poems and elicited from them keen lyricism,
shocking by fierce protest. Bernard Smith, in his authoritative
work on *European Vision and The South Pacific*, approves of
Byron's imaginative projection of Neuha, his Polynesian
Princess: she and Queequeg in *Moby Dick* are 'literary conventions, but they are conventions within which it was possible
for poet and novelist to go much farther in their endeavour to
understand the native and the native point of view'.

Farther, that is, than was permitted by the eighteenth-
century stereotype of the Noble Savage, present in Parny's
poems as in Diderot's *Supplement to Bougainville's Voyage*. By
the early nineteenth century, missionaries, professionally
committed to writing about and depicting pagans as ignoble,
had created a potent pejorative rhetoric. In the hands of the
evangelical poet James Montgomery, in his *Pelican Island*
(1827), the ignoble savage looks not altogether unlike Byron's
corsairs and Turks

> Their features terrible; when roused to wrath
> All evil passions lightened through their eyes . . .
> Their visages at rest were winter clouds
> Fix'd gloom, whence sun nor shower could be foretold:
> But, in high revelry, when full of prey,
> Cannibal prey, tremendous was the laughter.

Smith argues that the *romantic* savage, in poetry, fiction and

art, drew valuably on both the 'noble' and the 'ignoble'
stereotypes. The romantic savage combines a love of freedom and a devoted patriotism with a temperament reacting 'violently and immediately to experience.' He is brave,
emotionally profound, childlike, warmly generous. Smith
shows how such a convention could be related to the cult of the
Greeks which Byron promoted and exemplified. The artist
Augustus Earle, travelling in the Antipodes in the late 1820s,
despised Australian aborigines as 'the last link in the great
chain of existence which unites man with the monkey', but
thought the Polynesian Maoris perfectly beautiful; they re-
minded him of the Greeks of Homer's day, standing on the
threshold of a glorious future. In the same year another
traveller, D'Urville – the very Frenchman who had persuaded
the French government to buy the Venus de Milo when
stationed in the Aegean on survey work in 1820 – compared
the Maori *pa* with the Greek *polis* and meditated on the
succession of races which had emerged from obscurity to play
brilliant roles on the world stage. Once Gauls and Britons –
now Russians and North Americans – next, perhaps, Maoris
united by a great lawgiver.[13]

The comparison of savage and Greek went back at least as
far as J.J. Winckelmann's *Thoughts on the Imitation of Greek
Works in Painting and Sculpture*, an influential text translated
from German to English by Henry Fuseli in 1765 just as, not
wholly by coincidence, 'Ossian' was beginning to make
an impact. Winckelmann thought that the lithely athletic
American Indian was a living equivalent of Homer's Achilles.
The Greeks followed nature in their dress. Their arts imitated nature and were characterised by 'noble simplicity'.[14]
Byron echoes Winckelmann when writing about the Apollo
Belvedere in *Childe Harold* (Canto IV CLXI-CLXIII). He
might seem in *The Island* to echo Robert Wood's *Essay on the
Original Genius and Writings of Homer* (1769), which declared
that 'while manners were rude, when arts were little culti-
vated and before science was reduced to general principles,
poetry had acquired a greater degree of perfection than it has
ever since obtained'.[15] For this is what Byron says in Canto the
Second, Stanza V after Neuha has rendered her 'song of

Toobonai'. A 'simple ballad' outweighs in effect the monuments of empire:

> . . . The first, the freshest bud of Feeling's soil.
> Such was this rude rhyme – rhyme is of the rude –
> But such inspired the Norseman's solitude
> Who came and conquer'd: such, wherever rise
> Lands which no foes destroy or civilise
> Exist: and what can our accomplish'd art
> Of verse do more than reach the awaken'd heart?

C.M. Woodhouse has suggested that Byron's greatest gift
to the pan-European philhellenic movement was to get
people interested in *modern* Greeks, in people as well as
antiquities. He studied their literature and refuted the
views that it was non existent and that their speech was
debased. He befriended them while remaining cheerfully
ready to acknowledge their human failings.[16] What is involved
in his treatment of Torquil and Neuha on the one hand, and
Fletcher Christian on the other, is an ideological manoeuvre of
great complexity. He invokes an ideal antique Greece and
conveys it, via British and Polynesian figures, to the aid of
the freedom struggle of living Greeks in 1822. Scotland,
Gaeldom, Norse-ness, I submit, are there as a lubricant, rather
than for their own sake, though they facilitate, besides
Philhellenism, the exploration of other themes which preoccu-
pied Byron.

In the first Canto, Byron's 'antithetical mind' sets up a
complexly paradoxical relationship between the mutineers in
general and the conception of a golden age. Amplifying cues
from Bligh, Byron sees them as attracted back to Tahiti by 'the
care of some soft savage', and by the liberty and equality
possible in a society without money, a '. . . general garden,
where all steps may roam/Where Nature owns a nation as her
child.' We notice that, as in Byron's praise of primitive song,
a notion of progress is subtly admitted – such a notion as
D'Urville played with in New Zealand. The Norsemen, inspired by 'rude song', came and conquered, carrying world
history forward. Tahiti is a child *nation*.

The British mutineers are conquerors, but from a corrupted

civilisation. The island is 'gentle', but these men are 'wild' and seek 'repose' through other's 'woes', when they expel Bligh and his companions naked on to the boundless ocean. Christian's dreadful reply to Bligh – 'I am in hell! In hell!' – shows that like Conrad the Corsair, or Alp the renegade besieging Corinth, he represents a quasi-heroic mentality torn by the conflict between conscience and will – 'volumes lurked below his fierce farewell.' However, the will to return to the island of kindly Nature, 'the goldless age where gold disturbs no dreams', as Tahiti was before Europeans 'bestow'd their customs' and 'left their vices', is presented at the Canto's end as paradoxically positive: 'And yet they seek to nestle with the dove/And tame their fiery spirits down to love.'

In the second Canto we find that Neuha and Torquil have achieved a love which represents an ideal fusion of European and Tahitian values, but on the basis of similar childhood conditioning by seas and mountains. Neuha is 'in years a child' though 'in growth a woman'; she is voluptuous yet faithful, energetic but selfless. Torquil has 'taught her passion's desolating joy' – the lovers are suspended until the end of the poem in the ecstasy of love's early stages, but this, as readers of *Don Juan* know, cannot last. Neuha is innocent as a lake before an earthquake arrives to

. . . tear the naiad's cave,
Root up the spring, and trample on the wave
And crush the living waters to a mass,
The amphibious desert of the dank morass.
And must their fate be hers? The eternal change
But grasps humanity with quicker range
And they who fall but fall as worlds will fall,
To rise, if just, a spirit o'er them all.

I am intrigued by the way in which Byron flirts with Christianity in that last line, and would be interested to see an interpretation of the poem in terms of the intimations of immortality which it proffers. [17] But here I am concerned with what he does with Scotland.

Torquil, being 'Hebridean', is attuned to mountains and wind. He is naturally bold – if born in Arabia he would have

been a rover, if fixed in Chile, a proud Indian chief – and 'On
Hellas' mountains, a rebellious Greek . . .'. But this very
energy, had he been 'bred to a throne', might have made him
unfit to reign; it is admirable in its place, even when seizing
thrones, but preys on itself if 'rear'd' to rule. Torquil represents the human capacity and appetite for power:

> A soaring spirit, ever in the van,
> A patriot hero or despotic chief,
> To form a nation's glory or its grief.

Here on Toobonai he has momentarily been *tamed* by Neuha,
into 'a blooming *boy*, a truant mutineer.'

We can now return to my opening quotation. Neuha and
Torquil are both *'children* of the isles'. Byron in youth had
written that curiously viable lyric which begins 'I would I were
a careless *child*/Still dwelling in my mountain *cave*.' Now he
associates his own early Highland memories on the one hand
with the fragile happiness of Torquil and Neuha – 'the half
savage and the whole'; on the other with the sublime scenes of
Greece which he can still behold with 'infant rapture' because
of his early love of mountains. So far Greece represents *nature*,
which taught Byron to 'adore' its landscapes. A few stanzas on
he plays with nature-worship – 'who thinks of self when
gazing on the sky?' – which would seem quasi-Wordsworthian,
did not Byron connect this with the carnal ecstasy of the
devoted lover.

Byron had been writing *Juan* for years and was wholly
practiced in his 'Juanist' poetic personality, which permitted him to move rapidly between the loftiest romantic
sentiment and the coarsest cynicism. *The Island* differs from
earlier exotic tales in that it contains 'Juanist' transitions. A
bluff English sailor's tobacco wafts into paradise, and an
English voice calls 'what cheer', Ben Bunting has come to warn
Torquil that a British ship has arrived to apprehend the
mutineers. And Torquil at once reacts with Gaelic-Norse
martial valour:

> '. . . We will die at our quarters like true men'.
> 'Ey, ey! for that 'tis all the same to Ben.'

Torquil appeals to Neuha:

> '. . . Unman me not; the hour will not allow
> A tear; I'm thine whatever intervenes!'
> 'Right' quoth Ben; 'that will do for the marines.'

Byron's note here reads: 'That will do for the marines but the sailors won't believe it is an old saying.' Ben's colloquial understatements, and his prosaic pipe, make Torquil's heroics seem ridiculous. A canto which starts in the Golden Age ends in bathos. What is Byron up to?

Well, if his practices work – and some might question whether they do – the effect is to modernise and humanise the fierce, 'half-savage' will for action and power which Torquil represents, and which is needed to free present-day Greece. The other mutineers have been 'crushed, dispers'd or ta'en' by the time the third Canto opens, but Torquil, Ben and Jack Skyscrape are still at large with Fletcher Christian. In an impressively sombre passage, intensely 'Byronic' as opposed to 'Juanist' we are told that the clubs and spears of their native allies have been useless against British guns; purely 'savage' courage, even that of Homer's heroes, cannot prevail in the present day.

> Even Greece can boast but one Thermopylae,
> Till now, when she has forged her broken chain
> Back to a sword, and dies and lives again!

Thermopylae will recur in the fourth Canto. When Torquil has safely escaped, thanks to to his Princess, to the secret cave, his three comrades make their last stand:

> '. . . and with that gloomy eye,
> Stern and sustain'd, of man's extremity,
> When hope is gone, nor glory's self remains
> To cheer resistance against death or chains, –
> They stood, the three, as the three hundred stood
> Who dyed Thermopylae with holy blood.
> But, ah! how different! 'tis the *cause* makes all,
> Degrades or hallows courage in its fall.

O'er them no fame, eternal and intense,
Blazed through the clouds of death and beckon'd hence;
No grateful country, smiling through her tears,
Begun the praises of a thousand years . . .

They will not be immortalised in Homeric epic, nor even perhaps in 'songs of Toobonai'. Christian, conscious of shame and guilt though he is, remains defiant till his last shot is expended, then plunges from a cliff and his body is 'crush'd into one gory mass', an inhuman shapelessness.

Torquil and Neuha live on to feast with the chiefs of 'the yet infant world'. We know from Byron that childlike love, like the primitive spear, is doomed to fail, the first for existential, the second for historical reasons. But Greece can be freed if virtues of the Romantic Savage – selflessness, patriotism, courage – can be wedded to animal tenacity like Christian's, and will to power like Torquil's. The guilt-making *violence* required for success will be sanctified by the primitive innocence displayed at an extreme in the 'childhood cave'. The freshness of natural man is endowed to the cause of Hellas by deft ideological elision. Torquil is a convenient agency for this gift, evoking Ossian's heroes and the courage of Highlanders at Culloden: the Gael transformed from doomed Noble Savage to potentially world-sweeping Romantic Savage (or Highland Soldier, helpful at Waterloo). Byron's ideological sleight could be summed up like this:

Ancient Greeks were romantic savages launching from Golden Age into triumphant nationhood with patriotic heroism, in the era of chariots and spears.

They dwelt with sea and mountains common to the formation of Polynesian and Gaelic-Norse Scot and their values: the narrator, claiming his own share of mountains, is the reader's window on to the landscapes of modern Greece, where mountain-sea, heroic-patriotic values are innate or latent.

Neuha's selfless (and triumphant) love represents innocence, will to sacrifice. This is a necessary ingredient in a heroic cause . . .

But so is Torquil's tenacious will to power, allied till almost the last with Christian's untameable animal courage, not yet perverted, however, by Christian's anti-social self-consciousness and psychic torment.

Torquil connects in turn with the bluff martial competence of the modern British tar, Ben Bunting . . . Whose appreciation of tobacco is shared by the narrator . . . The latter's ardour for the Greek cause is therefore not that merely of a feckless romantic. But he sees that the Homeric valour and innate patriotism of the savage are necessary to ennoble and inspire the struggle.

I wrote of Byron's 'tartanry' for shorthand purposes. He takes Scott's successful (*Lady of the Lake*) romanticisation of Gaeldom off on his own, libertarian route. He may have despised tartan. *The Age of Bronze*, the topical satire which he had just finished when he began *The Island*, ends with raucous merriment over Sir William Curtis, London Alderman, donning the tartan on his trip to Edinburgh with George IV – that royal visit which Scott stage managed. MacDiarmid could hardly have been sharper:

> My muse 'gan weep, but, ere a tear was spilt,
> She caught Sir William Curtis in a kilt!
> While throng'd the chiefs of every Highland clan
> To hail their brother, Vich Ian Alderman!
> Guildhall grows Gael, and echoes with Erse roar
> While all the Common Council cry 'Claymore!'
> Too see proud Albyn's tartans as a belt
> Gird the gross sirloin of a city Celt,
> She burst into a laughter so extreme,
> That I awoke – and lo! it was *no* dream!

But a touch of Ossian made it possible for Byron to transcend the fatalistic *impasse* of the wonderful Haidée episode in *Don Juan*.

Haidée's rescue of Juan and their free, quasi-childlike love prefigure the Neuha-Torquil relationship. Her father's combination of piracy with patriotism anticipates the collusion of raw energy with a good cause which *The Island* will implicitly advocate. 'Valour was his and beauty dwelt with her' – and both, Byron tells us, are celebrated in 'rude' song. But Haidée's death from horror and grief makes it hard to fuse her natural generosity with a successful, modern, heroic cause. The resourceful Neuha survives, having negotiated the first phase of coming to terms with modern reality in the era of triumphant commercial imperialism. Moral suspense is not resolved, unless by sleight of hand: Torquil's energy remains ambiguous, and Byron refuses to judge whether Christian has gone to hell. But neither libertarian belligerence nor natural heroism have been undermined. The option of idealistic struggle for nationhood remains open. Though we know by the end of the poem that 'civilisation' since 1790 has destroyed Polynesian Golden Age values, these are directed, along with those of Homer and 'Ossian', towards battle with the oppressive modern Turk.

NOTES

1. *Byron's Letters and Journals*, ed. Leslie A. Marchand, (1973–), vol. 10, 156.
2. Tom Scott, 'Byron as a Scottish Poet' in A. Bold (ed), *Byron: Wrath and Rhyme*, (1983), 17–37.
3. *BLJ*, vol. 2, 376–7.
4. Roderick S. Speer, *Studies in Scottish Literature XIV* (Columbia, South Carolina), 196–206.
5. Bernard Blackstone, *Byron III: Social Satire, Drama and Epic* (1971), 43.
6. M.G. Cooke, *The Blind Man Traces the Circle* (1969), 211.
7. *BLJ*, vol. 10, 89–90, 117–118.
8. William Bligh, *A Voyage to the South Sea . . .*, London: George Nicol, 1792 edn. 154ff.
9. Ibid., 162.
10. I follow the careful, demythologising account of the Mutiny in Gavin Kennedy's *Bligh*, 1978.
11. Sir John Barrow, *The Eventful History of the Mutiny and Piratical Seizure of HMS Bounty* (London, 1831), 88–9.
12. John Martin MD, *An Account of the Natives of the Tonga Islands . . .*, (Edinburgh, 1827, 3rd edition), I, 216–224.
13. Bernard Smith, *European Vision and the South Pacific* (1985, 2nd edition), 317–332.
14. Lorenz Eitner, ed. *Neoclassicism and Romanticism 1750–1830* (1971), I, 4–13.

15. Quoted in Hugh Honour, *Neo-Classicism* (1968), 64.
16. C.M. Woodhouse, *The Philhellenes* (1969), 10, 40–45.
17. There are others in 1:6, 2:16, 4:1, 4:3–4, 4:6; the association of the secret cave with the grave (its exterior) and a Gothic church (interior) reinforces this element, and could be seen as a key to the whole poem.

Byron landing from a Boat

MICHAEL REES

The only illustration to Moore's life of Byron in 1830 was an engraving of Sanders' oil painting, which shows Byron landing from a dinghy. This portrait, probably begun in 1807 when the poet was nineteen (as Moore's caption indicates), has contributed greatly to his image as a Romantic wanderer. Attended by Robert Rushton, the 'little page' of *Childe Harold's Pilgrimage*, Canto I, and son of a tenant at Newstead Abbey, Byron gazes defiantly and moodily into the distance, personifying the future Harold or Byronic hero, against a background of sea and cliffs which suggest the Highlands of Scotland.[1]

Artist and subject alike had Scottish origins. George Sanders (1774–1846) was born at Kinghorn, Fife, and educated in Edinburgh, but went to London in 1805 and became fashionable among the nobility: by 1806 he already had to refuse sitters. Byron, whom he painted several times, apparently commissioned the portrait of himself alone in 1807. A full-length engraving of this formed the frontispiece to the Moore-Wright collected edition of Byron in 1832, although W. Finden's *Illustrations of the Life and Works of Lord Byron* in 1834 included only a half-length engraving 'at the age of 17'. The poet might not have approved. In 1812 he made John Murray destroy a poor engraving from a Sanders miniature of him, intended for a new edition of *Childe Harold*, since 'the frontispiece of an author's visage is but a paltry exhibition'.[2]

In April 1809 Byron brought Rushton to London. It was doubtless then, at the studio in Vigo Lane[3], that Sanders completed the painting, perhaps copied from the earlier version, and added Rushton beside a dinghy with a larger boat behind and water, steep rocks, and clouds.

Byron had left Scotland in 1798 at the age of ten and never

151

returned, although *The Records of Invercauld* quote the gillie who claimed to have accompanied him to the summit of Lochnagar in 1803[4]. In August 1807 Byron revived his plan to revisit Scotland; he would travel to Edinburgh by carriage, tour the Highlands and take a boat to the Hebrides.[5] Nothing came of these plans, but a nostalgic allusion to them and to the days of 'Auld Lang Syne' may have lain behind his instructions to Sanders. Before leaving England for the Levant with John Cam Hobhouse in June 1809, Byron paid 250 guineas for the work, a canvas measuring 44½ by 35⅛ inches. By 1811 this was Sanders' standard fee for a full-length portrait.[6]

In letters to his mother from Falmouth, Constantinople and Greece, Byron referred five times to the painting, forever expected from Sanders, 'a noted limner'.[7] At last Catherine Gordon Byron announced its arrival 'after a *great* deal of trouble. Saunders [sic] said he kept it to show as an honor and credit to him, the countenance is *angelic* and the finest I ever saw and it is very like. Miss Rumbold (Sir Sidney Smith's Daughter in law) . . . fell quite in love with it . . .'[8] Byron's supposed letter to his mother of 1 July 1810, stating that the Sanders portrait 'does not *flatter* . . . but the subject is a bad one', is a forgery.[9] During Hobhouse's return journey from Greece, where he had left Byron in July 1810, he wrote to the latter from Cadiz: 'General Graham commander in chief here has seen your full length at Saunder's [sic] – he was praising it very much indeed – I could not help saying ["] I am glad you like that picture so much for it is mine" – which you know it is, for you gave it me . . .'[10] Here was a further Scottish link; Thomas Graham (1748–1843), later Baron Lynedoch, had come to Cadiz as lieutenant-governor to command the British defence troops.

Mrs Byron died in 1811, but when Newstead Abbey was sold abortively to Thomas Claughton in 1812–4 the Sanders painting was still there, since Byron's butler, 'old Joe' Murray, packed it up and kept it dry and 'in great perfection'.[11] In due course Hobhouse received the picture, of which a greatly inferior copy still hangs at Newstead. It was inherited in 1869 by his eldest daughter Charlotte, Lady Dorchester, who bequeathed it in 1914 to King George V. Part of the Royal

Collection since then, the Sanders portrait was lent by H.M.
The Queen for the important Byron exhibition at the Victoria
and Albert Museum in 1974.[12]

NOTES

1. See also David Piper, *The Image of the Poet: British Poets and
   their Portraits* (1982), 127.
2. Letter to John Murray, 23 October 1812. *Byron's Letters and
   Journals*, ed. Leslie A. Marchand (1973–82), vol. 2, 234.
3. Letter to Mrs Catherine Gordon Byron, 24 May 1810. *BLJ*,
   vol. 1, 243. The Sanders portrait is the colour frontispiece in
   this volume.
4. The Revd John Grant Michie, M.A., Minister of Dinnet, *The
   Records of Invercauld 1547–1827* (Aberdeen, 1901), 389.
5. Letter to Elizabeth Bridget Pigot, 11 August 1807. *BLJ*, vol.
   1, 131–2.
6. Geoffrey Wills, 'A Forgotten Scottish Painter', *Country Life*
   (8 October 1953), 1120.
7. From Falmouth, 22 June 1809 (*BLJ*, vol. 1, 206); from
   Constantinople, 24 May and 28 June 1810 (ibid., 243, 251);
   from Athens, 20 July, and Patras, 2 October 1810 (*BLJ*, vol.
   2, 4,18).
8. Doris Langley Moore, *Lord Byron: Accounts Rendered* (1974),
   129.
9. *BLJ*, vol. 1, 272.
10. *Byron's Bulldog: The Letters of John Cam Hobhouse to Lord
    Byron*, ed. Peter W. Graham (1984), 52.
11. D. L. Moore, op. cit., 473.
12. Anthony Burton and John Murdoch, *Byron: An exhibition to
    commemorate the 150th anniversary of his death* (1974), 9.
    (Exhibit A41.)

On Singing 'Dark Lochnagar'

SHEENA BLACKHALL

I must be one of the few Scots who came to learn of the connection between Dark Lochnagar and George Gordon Byron by reading it on a tea-towel in a Ballater gift shop. Until then, I had assumed (by the number of Deesiders who sang it, who'd never heard of Byron) that it was a traditional North-East ballad, rising from the common ancestral pool, best sung at 5 a.m. on a Hogmanay morning, on looking proudly and blearily at the mountain from any one of a number of Deeside cottar windows, mid-down a bottle of the whisky of that name.

My father could never cross the Border without breaking into a rendition of Dark Lochnagar, with the verve of Bruce accosting de Bohun from the stirrups, axe raised, with a heavy emphasis on 'England, thy beauties are tame and domestic' – lest we were in danger of forgetting the fact. For of course, Lochnagar is our family property, grudgingly shared with others of Deeside extraction, Byron included (his maternal bloodline dips back to Aboyne), and nobody else's business.

Beside it, other mountains wither into inconsequence. I know this, having travelled – not extensively, but travelled none the less – in places as diverse as Europe, England and Fraserburgh.

I found the Eiger as cold and moth-eaten as Miss Havisham's inedible wedding-cake. I found it as populous as downtown Shanghai, its *pistes* traffic-jammed with tourists, its snow as shop-soiled as Woolworths' floor after a sale. I thought it crude Kentucky moonshine, chocolate-box saccharine, a phallic meringue of a mountain, which promised great things but whose ecstasies were small. On its lower slopes, the noblest beast it could boast was a curly-topped Swiss cow,

looking remarkably like a Heidi-Shirley-Temple, ringing its
bell like a till opening and shutting incessantly.

In Ireland, try as I might, I couldn't find *any* mountains,
merely a quilt of soggy green mammaries. 'The Irish', Father
remarked as the guide extolled in song the umpteenth
supposed beauty spot, 'will sing about *onything!*' Whereas we,
of course, were particular. We sang about Lochnagar. Norman
MacCaig once said that God was Mozart when he wrote Cul
Mor. I have news for him. Lochnagar *is* Mozart.

But fancy George Gordon writing the song, Mistress Gordon of Gight's 'Crooked Deevil'! For years Crutchie Geordie,
or Lord Byron, to give him his English title, was the moody,
frozen man on the plinth outside my brother's school, whom
my mother nodded to, never omitting to mutter 'Byron'
conversationally as we trotted past. Not once did he have the
good manners to reply. As a very small child, I remember
thinking that extremely rude, and wondering why he let
pigeons sit on his head, and did he ever get down to stretch his
legs and walk about a bit?

Later, I discovered that Byron climbed my Lochnagar in the
summer of 1803, from Invercauld, going by the Garrawalt
Glen, by the crags of Loch an Uan, resting frequently but,
typically, rejecting help. It wasn't his first sight of the
mountain, he was familiar with it from the age of eight, from
holidays at Ballaterach.

From the age of nothing onwards, I too spent summers on
Deeside. By the time I was eight, I had officially adopted
Lochnagar as my big brother cum playmate. I was always
pleased to see him, and I was sure the joy was reciprocal; we
spent hours of fun together in all weathers. Every night, before
dropping off to sleep, I would say my round of 'goodnights' as
only children and 'The Waltons' do, and always ended with
'Goodnight Lochnagar, goodnight Dee', because you should
never omit your friends.

I grew very possessive of my mountain, and was rude and
discourteous to the assortment of Japanese, American and
people from Middlesbrough who asked directions to him. I
would feign complete ignorance of English, and give incom-

prehensible replies in deepest Doric, throwing in a string of
Gaelic oaths I had learned from an Inverness cousin of poor
moral fibre. Later still, when behind the wheel of a car, I would
pretend to be ignorant of passing places, and block the
winding, tendril-thin road to give a quick paean of song to my
friend, a chorus or two of Dark Lochnagar in his honour, thus
obliging the Dutch, Hindi, Zulu, English or whatever to veer
off the road into a bog, or reverse eight miles and go home,
wherever home was.

For of course he is no mere mountain, he's also a panacea,
the family medicine-chest. When any of us fell ill, my father
would listen indulgently to the doctor's diagnosis and as soon
as he left would say, 'Whit they *really* need's a wee whiff o'
Lochnagar!' And a whiff of Lochnagar we would get. And
what's more, it worked!

I like a piece of my mountain by me. It's nice to have friends
near at hand. I squeeze my little Lochnagar stone when I'm
anxious, and I squeeze it for comfort when I'm sad. It's the
most valuable thing I own.

So, when I sing Dark Lochnagar, I don't sing for an
audience. I don't sing for Byron, and I certainly don't sing for
myself. When I sing Dark Lochnagar, you see, I'm singing for a
friend.

Afterword

J. DRUMMOND BONE

Perhaps there is room for an afterword of gentle Byronic scepticism. The papers of this volume have as their reason for being a project to characterise Byron's Scottishness. I rather wonder if in the event they even try to do that in any very serious way. What I really wonder is whether this project could ever be anything more than a 'design-governing-posture', a useful fiction with which to compose one's thoughts. If there is a connecting tissue in what has gone before, and I do sense one, it seems to me rather to be the issue of Byron's political seriousness. National identity is a difficult and slippery concept, and there are dangers for both the object of thought and the thinker in its invocation. Byron's idea of nationality had not had to be tested by the consequences of the organic mysticism which was to invoke his name only a few years after his death. Perhaps too these consequences are never tested by the nationalism of a relatively small country such as Scotland, which can therefore afford to indulge itself – it is nationalism by opposition rather than by assumption. But all this is truism. The point which this collection begins to make almost against its own will is that Byron's characteristic way of being Byron is never serious enough to be dangerous by way of abstract identities, whether these are national or political. It *is* unserious enough to be wildly dangerous to those who think in terms of discrete identities, essences, purities, and polarities. Its unseriousness consists, for a start, in its inability not to be serious. Byron and his poetry refuse the dialectic of serious and unserious – and this is deeply worrying for those who believe they have a privileged access either to the serious or to the cynical.

It is entirely characteristic that Byron's so-called 'Luddite Song' has not yet been published *as it was written* outside of editions of Byron's letters. For *pace* David Craig it was not suppressed until six years after his death – for fear of its Luddite subversiveness – but has effectively been suppressed until this day, and regrettably one has to include McGann's edition in this suppression, because it subverts a deeper decorum of seriousness and cynicism, of the politically committed and the personally scurrilous. The three stanzas of the Luddite song are bracketed by two other stanzas in the letter in which they occur, but in order to leave this poem as distinct and unambiguous they are conveniently displaced in all 'editions'. These are the stanzas beginning: 'What are you doing now,/Oh Thomas Moore . . . Sighing or suing now,/ Rhyming or wooing now . . . /Which Thomas Moore?' It is really 'not on' to appropriate Byron to a political identity, and then to blame him for not living up to it. But this stubborn refusal to be appropriated is uncomfortable – highly so.

But of course there is a different kind of unseriousness too, the opportunistic unseriousness of which Andrew Noble writes – the Byron cynically exploiting the market Scott had created for the sensationalist tale. That there is an element of escapist mannerism in these is difficult to deny. There have been recent attempts, notably by Daniel Watkins in *Byron's Eastern Tales* and by Marilyn Butler and Jerome McGann to read these as political allegories, or near allegories. Even if one is convinced by these arguments it would be impossible to say that the poems were redeemed by this however, since it has gone almost totally unrecognized from their publication until now. But are we not being misled by another impulse to impose unity on the man who 'must contradict himself on every page'? If these contradictions were easy, if they were always in the control of the writer, they would not really *be* contradictions. The 'mobility' of which Byron writes in *Don Juan* XVI is a 'most painful and unhappy attribute' – though witnesses to it can be misled by its seeming 'facility'. The honest writer, Byron seems to mean, does not even write his own contradictoriness, rather he is written by it. And that 'honest' can be misleading too, for the honest writer will also be written by his own dishonesties. To be committedly in bad

faith is part of the cant of consistency. This is not to defend the
Turkish Tales from a charge of literary expediency. On the
contrary, I feel that to attempt the defence is to interpret in bad
faith if the defence is the discovery of a unified allegorical
politics, while on the other hand, if the attack on these poems
is seen as a description of some 'core' failing in Byron or his
poetry, then this too is to avoid the difficulty of living
inconsistently. It is difficult again to accept what Byron enacts
– that consistency and total moral seriousness is *easier* and
more cynical than inconsistency and moral dubiety.

Am I attributing a Romantic view of unity to my colleagues
in this book when in fact they would disown it, and claim that
particular politics or particular nationality have no essential
quality in their usage? Perhaps. It would indeed be a Romantic
view of language if we said that words themselves were
reductionist. But it is also a characteristic of Romanticism to
will the infinite into the particular, and thereby to envalue the
word (while arguably silencing it). It might be inaccurate
therefore to say simply that a national identity reduces the
person – this would only be true if we believed the person to be
a being greater than his or her historical self, and if we believed
that we are also likely to believe that national identity is greater
than the historical nation. The failure of words depends on the
expectations laid on them. On the other hand not to realise the
reductionist possibility is not to have any expectations of
insight. But then once again is it perhaps wrong to feel that the
project of identity is surreptitiously always transcendent? But
if it is not, why is it so important to those who follow it? *Is* there
a way out of all this? Perhaps the whole game of paths through
identities to higher levels of being, or of the reduction of these
higher levels through the discriminations of words, is not one
which Byronists should really play, either for or against. If we
love him, we should let him be – certainly not ourselves in
nation or politics, not accountable to our understanding of the
serious or the cynical – 'only' someone whose voice we fondly
hear.

Index